Love v. Regency

Third Edition

LOVE V. REGENCY

Third Edition

Denitsa R. Mavrova Heinrich
Rodney & Betty Webb Associate Professor of Law
University of North Dakota School of Law

Edward R. Stein, JD
Adjunct Professor of Law
University of Michigan Law School

and

Jonathan Rest, MD

NITA®
NATIONAL INSTITUTE FOR TRIAL ADVOCACY

Address inquiries to:
Reprint Permission
National Institute for Trial Advocacy
325 W. South Boulder Rd., Ste. 1
Louisville, CO 80027-1130
Phone: (800) 225-6482
Email: publications@nita.org

ISBN 979-8-88669-021-7
FBA 2021
eISBN 979-8-88669-022-4
eFBA 2022

Printed in the United States of America

ASPEN PUBLISHING

Official co-publisher of NITA.
aspenpublishing.com/NITA

Contents

Acknowledgments

We would like to extend our profound thanks to Brady Carpenter and Ryan Zetterholm of Ankura Consulting Group, LLC, who spent many hours reviewing and updating the financial information and expert reports. They went above and beyond in their assistance. This case file wouldn't be the same without their help.

CASE SUMMARY

Dr. Stanley Love is a Central City dermatologist. For more than a decade, Dr. Love has performed cosmetic surgery in addition to his general dermatology practice. Since YR-13, he has marketed his cosmetic surgery practice with "The Love Look" as his slogan. Dr. Love did not register the slogan with any state agency or with the U.S. Patent and Trademark Office.

In mid-YR-13, two New York City plastic surgeons formed Regency Plastic Surgery, PC. In YR-12, Regency registered the service mark, "The Look of Love," with the U.S. Patent and Trademark Office and began using the slogan in all its marketing. Over the years, Regency expanded its market area by purchasing plastic surgery practices in communities beyond New York City.

In YR-6, Regency purchased a plastic surgery practice in Oakdale, a well-to-do suburb located twenty-five miles north of Central City. Regency began using "The Look of Love" in its marketing campaign in the Central City area. Central City has a population of about 750,000; the metropolitan area has a population of about 1,400,000.

In early YR-1, Dr. Love filed suit against Regency, alleging infringement of his common law trademark of "The Love Look" and seeking injunctive relief and damages. Regency denies liability, claiming Dr. Love had no common trademark because "The Love Look" is merely descriptive; therefore, Dr. Love could acquire no common law trademark rights in the slogan. Regency also claims that even if "The Love Look" has acquired trademark protection, Regency did not infringe the trademark. Finally, Regency asserts Dr. Love's claims are barred by laches and the statute of limitations.

Instructions for Use as a Full Trial

1. The plaintiffs and the defendant must call the two witnesses listed as that party's witnesses on the witness list.

2. All witness roles, except Dr. Love, are not gender specific. Dr. Love, however, is portrayed as male in the online advertisements and therefore it is recommended that Dr. Love be played by a person identifying as male.

3. All testifying witnesses who have identified the parties, other individuals, or tangible evidence in statements or prior deposition testimony must, if asked, identify the same at trial. Additionally, witnesses have knowledge of all documents on which their signatures appear.

4. Each witness testified previously and agreed under oath at the outset of their testimony to give a full and complete description of all material events that occurred and to correct the transcript of such testimony for inaccuracies and completeness before signing the deposition transcript.

5. All exhibits in the case file are authentic. In addition, each exhibit contained in the file is the original of that document unless otherwise noted on the exhibit or as established by the evidence.

6. All signatures are authentic. No advocate may attempt to impeach a witness by arguing that a signature on a transcript, statement, or exhibit does not comport with a signature or initials on any other exhibit.

7. Other than what is supplied in the problem itself, there is nothing exceptional or unusual about the background information of any of the witnesses that would bolster or detract from their credibility.

8. The case file is a "closed universe" of facts, and advocates may use only the materials in the file except where the file states otherwise.

9. "Beyond the record" shall not be entertained as an objection. Rather, advocates shall use cross-examination to impeach a witness about any material facts not contained in the case file. If asked, witnesses must admit that the fact to which they have testified is not in their statement or testimony.

10. The Statement of the Case cannot be used as evidence or for examination or cross-examination of any witness.

INSTRUCTIONS FOR USE AS A FULL TRIAL

[illegible]

Witness List:

The following witnesses must be called in this case:

For Plaintiffs:

Dr. Stanley Love
Casey Delp

For Defendant:

Dr. Drew Segan
Jamie Anderson

The expert witnesses in this file may be called as optional witnesses, but it is not necessary to call experts as witnesses to use the file. The reports may be admitted by stipulation if the experts are not called.

Procedural Matters

1. The Federal Rules of Evidence and Federal Rules of Civil Procedure apply.

2. The trial may relate to liability only or liability and damages. Verdict forms are provided for both.

3. All dispositive pretrial motions have been filed and denied; no further dispositive motions (other than motions for judgment as a matter of law) will be entertained.

Substantive Matters

1. The parties stipulate that the State of Nita has jurisdiction over this matter. No issues of jurisdiction or venue are pertinent to the case at hand.

2. All years in these materials are stated in the following form:

   a. YR-0 indicates the actual year in which the case is being tried (the present year);

   b. YR-1 indicates the next preceding year (please use the actual year);

   c. YR-2 indicates the second preceding year (please use the actual year), etc.

3. The applicable law is contained in the proposed jury instructions provided at the end of this case file.

4. Electronic copies of all exhibits can be found at the following website:

http://bit.ly/1P20Jea
Password: Love3

STATE COURT OF NITA
COUNTY OF NITA

STANLEY LOVE, MD and STANLEY LOVE, MD, PC, Plaintiffs, vs. REGENCY PLASTIC SURGERY, Defendant.	)	CIVIL NO. YR-1–CV–96369

COMPLAINT AND JURY DEMAND

Plaintiffs, for their complaint against the Defendant, allege:

1. Plaintiff, Stanley Love, MD, is a resident of the State of Nita and the sole owner of Plaintiff, Stanley Love, MD, PC, a professional corporation.

2. Dr. Love is a board-certified dermatologist and a trained cosmetic surgeon who practices dermatology and cosmetic surgery in the Central City, Nita, area.

3. Defendant, Regency Plastic Surgery, PC, is a New York corporation that is authorized to do business in the State of Nita.

4. Starting in YR-13 and continuing to date, Plaintiff Dr. Love has used the phrase "The Love Look" in marketing his cosmetic surgery practice in the Central City area.

5. By using "The Love Look," Dr. Love and his PC acquired common law trademark rights to "The Love Look" in connection with cosmetic surgery services in this state.

6. Starting in YR-6 and continuing to date, Regency has used the phrase "The Look of Love" to market its cosmetic surgery services in the Central City area.

7. Regency's use of "The Look of Love" infringes on Plaintiffs' trademark rights to "The Love Look."

8. Plaintiffs have been damaged by Defendant's infringement in an amount equal to Plaintiffs' lost income or Defendant's wrongful profit, whichever is greater.

9. Plaintiffs are entitled to treble damages because Defendant's infringement has been, and continues to be, willful.

As a result, Plaintiffs request:

a. damages in the amount of Plaintiffs' loss or Defendant's profit, whichever is greater;

b. trebled damages; and

c. a permanent injunction against Defendant's use of "The Look of Love."

Plaintiffs demand trial by jury.
Filed: 01/04/YR-1

QUAN, WARREN & ROTHSCHILD by:

Mickie Quan

Mickie Quan
400 S. Ashley Street
Central City, Nita 80144

STATE COURT OF NITA
COUNTY OF NITA

STANLEY LOVE, MD, et al.,	)	
	)	
Plaintiffs,	)	
	)	
vs.	)	CIVIL NO. YR-1–CV–96369
	)	
REGENCY PLASTIC SURGERY,	)	
	)	
Defendant.	)	
	)	

ANSWER

1. Neither admitted nor denied.
2. Neither admitted nor denied.
3. Admitted.
4. Neither admitted nor denied.
5. Defendant denies that "The Love Look" is subject to Plaintiffs acquiring any common law trademark rights because the phrase is merely descriptive of surgery performed by Dr. Stanley Love.
6. Defendant acknowledges that, since YR-6, it has made lawful use of its registered service mark, The Look of Love®, in marketing its plastic surgery services in the Central City area.
7. Denied.
8. Denied.
9. Denied.

AFFIRMATIVE DEFENSES

1. The six-year statute of limitations has expired on some or all of Plaintiffs' claims.
2. Plaintiffs' claims are barred by the doctrine of laches.
3. Plaintiffs have infringed Defendant's registered service mark and, therefore, come to court with unclean hands.

As a result, Defendant requests that this Court dismiss Plaintiffs' Complaint with prejudice and award costs to Defendant.

Defendant demands trial by jury.
Filed: 02/12/YR-1

KILPATRICK, STONE & SHAH by:

Alicia Robertson

Alicia Robertson
1400 Vernor Ave.
Central City, Nita 80144

STATE COURT OF NITA
COUNTY OF NITA

STANLEY LOVE, MD, et al.,	)	
	)	
Plaintiffs,	)	
	)	
vs.	)	CIVIL NO. YR-1–CV–96369
	)	
REGENCY PLASTIC SURGERY,	)	
	)	
Defendant.	)	
	)	

ANSWERS TO PLAINTIFFS' INTERROGATORIES AND REQUESTS FOR ADMISSIONS [excerpted]

Plaintiffs' Interrogatories to Defendant

Interrogatory #8: Please provide the name and address of all Regency Oakdale patients who obtained from Regency Oakdale the cosmetic surgery procedures listed on Exhibit 5, indicating for each patient which procedure(s) they obtained and the date(s) of the procedure(s).

Response #8: Defendant declines to respond and objects to this interrogatory because the information sought is privileged and confidential under both federal law (HIPAA) and state law providing for physician-patient privilege.

Plaintiffs' Requests for Admission

Request #3: Please admit that a preexisting state common law trademark takes precedence in this state over a trademark that is later registered with the U.S. Patent and Trademark Office.

Response #3: Admitted.

DEPOSITIONS

Deposition of Stanley Love, MD
January 9, YR-0

My name is Stanley Love, MD. I'm fifty-five years old. I graduated from Northern Illinois University in YR-33 and the University of Illinois School of Medicine in YR-28. I completed my dermatology training at the University of Michigan, after which I started working for Dr. Eric Brown. That's when we first moved to Central City. When Eric retired about twenty years ago, I took over his practice and incorporated it. The corporate name is Stanley Love, MD, PC. I've been in practice by myself ever since. I am board certified in dermatology and a fellow of the American Society of Cosmetic Surgery. No, I don't teach at any medical school. And, no, I'm not board certified in cosmetic surgery.

For the first ten years, my practice was very much like most derm practices. I did some surgery—biopsies, excisions, and other similar procedures—but I mostly did general dermatology. My favorite part, though, has always been surgery. I'm pretty good at it.

In the summer of YR-15, I took a course in eyelid surgery. After this course, I started doing eyelid surgery as part of my practice. I took some more courses in cosmetic surgery over the next several months. As I started doing more surgery in my practice, my primary care friends began referring patients to me, specifically for cosmetic surgery. No, I didn't have cosmetic surgery training as part of my residency, but I understand that derm residents get training in cosmetic surgery these days—eyelid surgery, Botox, liposuction, even facelifts. And, yes, the seminars I attended were all accredited by the American Academy of Cosmetic Surgery.

At the time, my wife, Bobbi, who is also my office manager, encouraged me to do more cosmetic surgery. She used to joke with my patients. When they'd come into the office, she'd ask them if they'd come for the "Look of Love." We decided it would be great to get more cosmetic surgery patients, and my wife talked to a friend who runs the ad agency downstairs in our building—it's called the Gamble Agency. He agreed to help us advertise the practice. No, we don't have a formal contract with Gamble. Ed Gamble warned us that because "The Look of Love" was a song title, there might be legal problems in using it in our advertising. So, we changed it to "The Love Look."

We came out with a brochure in the spring of YR-13. It has that logo on the front page—"The Love Look"—along with my picture. Yes, Exhibit 2 is the version of the brochure we've been using since about YR-4. Also in YR-13, we started to put ads in the paper. At first they were small, but by the end of the year, we were taking out one-eighth-page ads. We got a website at the same time, because everyone said we had to have one. We hired someone to design it, but I don't remember who. Exhibit 3 is a printout of my website. And then in YR-8, we started to advertise online. Exhibit 1 shows my online ad. We hired a production company to come in and film it, but they have gone out of business and I don't know where the owner is now. We considered radio, but Ed Gamble promised more bang for our buck if we went with online ads. He recommended I be in the ads myself, so we decided to go for it.

I remember the first time we filmed one of those ads. I was so nervous, I was shaking like a leaf. But it turned out to be no big deal. And then we did some more, and I got to like it. I was pretty good at it. We've made six or eight ads since we began. Now, new patients come in asking for "The Love Look." I remember the first time I heard it in public. Bobbi and I were at one of our favorite restaurants, and the couple at the next table was discussing cosmetic surgery. The wife said she wanted to go in for "The Love Look." We laughed at the time, but it became a really big deal. No, we never registered the slogan with the U.S. Patent and Trademark Office. We didn't know anything about that, and the Gamble people never mentioned anything about registering it either.

The online ads made a big difference. A lot more cosmetic surgery patients came in. Before we started advertising online, we used to see one or two new cosmetic surgical patients per week. By the end of YR-8, I had at least three times that many new patients. And they came in for the big procedures right off the bat—blephs (that's eyelid surgery to remove the sag), Botox, and lipo. Those ads were so successful that, early in YR-7, we decided to stop the newspaper ads and focus exclusively on online ads.

I do a lot of cosmetic procedures, including blepharoplasty, dermabrasion, filler injections like collagen, sclerotherapy, laser resurfacing, chemical peels, liposuction, and Botox. I hope to introduce mini-facelifts within the next year. As I said, my training for all of these procedures has been through the Cosmetics Institute. It's a training center in Chicago that offers all kinds of procedure workshops, which are approved by the American Academy of Cosmetic Surgery. I do most of these procedures in my office, though I do have privileges at the Central City Surgi-Center. It's been a while since I did a case at the Surgi-Center. I'd have to check my records to be sure. But I occasionally do go there. For example, if I have an elderly patient and want to have a nurse anesthetist with me when I operate, then I go to the Surgi-Center.

On September 4, YR-6, one of my patients told me about Regency. I remember the conversation as if it were yesterday. It was the day before my birthday. I was looking for a chart in the file when I heard my wife greet one of our regular patients on the phone with a joke about our online ad, as she often did. The patient wanted to make an appointment in our new Oakdale office. That stopped me dead in my tracks. My wife told her we don't have an office in Oakdale, which is twenty-five miles north of Central City; we have only one office. The patient said she had seen an ad in Central City Monthly for our Oakdale office. She was sure it was us because the ad used my name and slogan.

My wife and I Googled Oakdale and "The Love Look" right away. To our surprise, we found an ad for Regency. When we clicked on the link, we discovered "The Look of Love" and came to find out it was Drs. Connelly and Waters—two surgeons in Oakdale that I've known for a long time. They used to do mostly reconstructive work and a lot of burns. But now, they're a part of Regency and use a slogan that is almost identical to ours. And they're only doing cosmetics. Yes, I know they're not dermatologists. They're plastic surgeons, but the patient certainly didn't know that. As a matter of fact, she didn't even make an appointment with us that day. She said she would call back, but she didn't. Anyway, as you can imagine, I was very concerned about what I found out about Drs. Waters and Connelly. I didn't sleep very well that night.

Q. Did you do anything to express your concerns to Dr. Waters or Dr. Connelly?

A. Yes, of course.

Q. What did you do?

A. I called Dr. Waters three times over the next few days, but no one called me back.

Q. What messages, if any, did you leave?

A. I just asked for a call back.

When Dr. Waters didn't call back, I called my lawyer, Mickie Quan, to ask what I should do. Mickie suggested I write an email to Regency and ask them to stop using the slogan. I thought maybe they didn't even realize what they were doing, although, in retrospect, they knew full well what was going on. So, on September 13, I sent an email to Dr. Segan, the president of Regency. I asked that Regency stop using "The Look of Love" slogan. Yes, Exhibit 4 is the email I sent. Unfortunately, it didn't do any good. Dr. Segan emailed me back in October and said they wouldn't stop using the slogan. That it wouldn't make any difference because they don't advertise online. Dr. Segan also told me I shouldn't worry because they didn't plan to steal any of my derm patients. But that's rubbish. They've been stealing my patients ever since.

My income has fallen substantially because of Dr. Segan and Regency. At least 30 percent. In YR-6, my cosmetic surgery revenue was over $325,000. Last year, it fell down to $250,000. I'm certain that difference is attributable to a decrease in the number of cosmetic procedures I've been doing since Regency came to town. Yes, Exhibit 5 is the record of my cosmetic procedures and revenues from YR-8 through YR-1. We enter each procedure I perform and the actual income we receive into a program called Medisoft, which is a standard medical-financial program. The program generated the report. Our bookkeeper does the actual inputting, and she gets the program to generate whatever kind of report we need. No, I don't use the program myself, but I know it's been quite reliable and many doctors use it.

I've had several patients ask me if I was working with the Regency doctors. They thought that since they were using "The Look of Love" slogan, that we must be affiliated with them somehow. I even had to put a sign up in the office informing my patients we had nothing to do with Regency. A lot of our patients are still very confused about that. Yes, some of our patients have told us they called Regency by mistake to make appointments. When they called, Regency gave them our phone number. They had it right there, ready to give to our patients when they called. Can you imagine? They've known all along they were causing all this confusion, and yet, they continue to use our slogan.

Exhibit 11 is a printout of my website homepage. I had Ed Gamble add the warning that I'm not associated with any other medical practice right after I got Dr. Segan's email blowing off my concerns.

In late YR-2, I met a woman at a charity event who told me she meant to have eyelid surgery done by me. But, because of her confusion over Regency's ads, she made an appointment there instead. She wound up having the surgery done there and was very disappointed with the results.

Q. When did you first consider suing Regency?

A. In the spring, three years ago. Ed Gamble told me that, if he were me, he'd sue. I thought long and hard about it, but I decided not to.

Q. Why?

A. Because I don't like the idea of people suing each other, and I thought I could probably ride out the economic impact. But after my income kept on falling further down, I didn't really have much choice, did I?

Yes, I'll tell you what "The Love Look" is all about. It's about common sense. When my patients come in for "The Love Look," they know they're getting the surgery that's right for them. They know I'm not going to sell them a bill of goods just to get a surgical fee. I give them my promise that what I do will really make a difference in their lives. And they know that if I don't think the surgery is right for them, I won't do it. I have a book filled with letters from my cosmetic patients, thanking me for what I did. Word of mouth is really my best advertising. "The Love Look" is about trust—their trust in me and my good name.

No, I don't have any specific retirement plans. I love what I do, and I plan to keep doing it as long as I can. At some point, I suppose, I might hire an associate to cut down my time in the office a little. Yes, I'd like, eventually, to sell my practice to someone. That would provide retirement income.

I have read this transcript and certify it is an accurate transcription of my deposition testimony given on January 9, YR-0.

Stanley Love, MD

Dr. Stanley Love

Deposition of Casey Delp
January 11, YR-0

I'm Casey Delp. I'm forty-six years old, and I live at 1407 Whitehall Road in Oakdale. I'm the CFO of Homes Are Us, which is the largest residential real estate agency in this area. I have a bachelor's degree from Penn State and an MBA from Central City State. I'm married and have two sons, one in high school and one in college.

Dr. Love is my cosmetic surgeon. He's performed eyelid surgery on me, and I get regular Botox injections from him. I first saw him in YR-4. After thinking about cosmetic surgery for a couple of years, I finally decided to look into it. I'd seen Dr. Love's ad online, and he seemed like a very nice man. Plus, a friend of mine had gone to him and really liked him. Then, I saw an ad in Central City Monthly for what I thought was Dr. Love's Oakdale office. So, I called and made an appointment.

I thought the ad was for Dr. Love because it used his name and was for cosmetic surgery. I assumed it was Dr. Love. Exhibit 9 is either the ad I saw or something very much like it. Yes, the ad said "Regency Plastic Surgery," which I assumed was the name of Dr. Love's business.

Q. Did you specifically ask for an appointment with Dr. Love when you called Regency?

A. I can't really remember. I may have just asked for an evaluation for cosmetic surgery.

Q. Would you have used the term "cosmetic," as opposed to "plastic," surgery?

A. I could have used either. To me, they're the same.

No, I didn't know Dr. Love was a dermatologist when I made the call. I didn't learn that until I had my appointment at Regency. My appointment was scheduled for about a week after I called. I filled out some paperwork and talked to a nurse. Then, I talked to a doctor, who explained the types of procedures they could do. During that conversation, I asked if I would get to meet Dr. Love. The doctor I was talking to told me this was not Dr. Love's office. The doctor also said Dr. Love was a dermatologist, not a plastic surgeon, and I'd be much better off with a fully qualified plastic surgeon. I felt this was sort of a hard sell, so I said I'd think about everything and left.

I thought it was a hard sell because I was there to discuss facial procedures, and this guy was telling me about liposuction, body contouring, and tummy tucks. Way more than I was interested in. Plus, they sounded pretty negative about Dr. Love. I thought that was kind of unprofessional.

Within a couple of weeks, I actually saw Dr. Love. I found his number online and made an appointment. I really liked him. No hard sell at all. He explained what he could do and how much it would cost. He showed me some before and after pictures and told me to think about it and let him know if I wanted to go ahead with the procedure. I decided to go forward, and it went exactly as Dr. Love said it would.

Yes, Dr. Love did tell me I would have "The Love Look." As a matter of fact, he joked about that. And to tell you the truth, I do love the look that resulted.

I don't recall if, when I was at Regency's office, anyone mentioned "The Love Look" or "The Look of Love" or anything like that.

Yes, I guess the bottom line is that I got exactly what I wanted from exactly the doctor I wanted. But only after wasting two hours at Regency.

Yes, I continued to see Dr. Love, as I've said, for Botox, and one of my boys has seen him for acne. Dr. Love and his wife hired my firm as their realtor when they sold their house and bought a condo. He's also been very generous in supporting the annual Central City Hospice fundraising auction. For each of the last three years, he's donated $1,000 worth of Botox injections. I'm president of the hospice board of trustees, and I recruited Dr. Love's donations.

No, I've never socialized with Dr. Love or his wife except at the auction. They sit at our table.

No, Dr. Love didn't ask me to be a witness in this case. Actually, his wife did at the auction. She told me Regency has really screwed Dr. Love over, and I said I'd be happy to help if I could.

I have read this transcript and certify it is an accurate transcription of my deposition testimony given on January 11, YR-0.

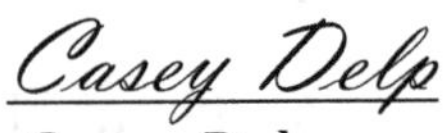

Casey Delp

Deposition of Drew Segan
January 12, YR-0

My name is Drew Segan, MD. I graduated from Cornell Medical School in YR-29. I then took a general surgery residency at Northwestern and a plastic surgery fellowship at the University of Pennsylvania, which I completed in YR-21. I'm board certified in both general surgery and plastics. I am an unpaid clinical associate professor at Columbia University School of Medicine. I don't teach formal classes, but I have plastic surgery fellows assigned to thirty-day rotations in our New York City office.

I now practice only nine months a year. I take three months off and devote one of those months to medical missionary work in East Africa. The great majority of that work is reconstructive surgery, about 60 percent with children and 40 percent with adults. The sponsor is DOC, Doctors Operating for Christ.

I am a shareholder in Regency Plastic Surgery, PC. I was president of the corporation from its founding in October YR-13 until October YR-3, when Dr. Dale Tremble, one of the younger New York City surgeons, took over. We have sixteen shareholders, all of whom are Regency surgeons. We also employ six nonshareholder surgeons, many nurses and physician assistants, and of course clerical and business personnel. I can't give you exact numbers for each because staffing changes all the time.

After I completed my fellowship, I was hired by Fedele and Levine, a New York plastic surgery partnership. Drs. Fedele and Levine were the partners, and Dr. Terry Fostyk and I were employees. We eventually became partners and took over the practice in YR-13, when Drs. Fedele and Levine retired. We purchased their interests over ten years. We incorporated as Regency Plastic Surgery, PC, with each of us owning 50 percent of the stock.

Q. What changes did you make after taking over the practice thirteen years ago?

A. The old practice was traditional plastic surgery, with about 40 percent reconstructive surgery, accident injuries, burns, and the like. The other 60 percent was elective cosmetic surgery. Terry and I decided to transition as quickly as possible to 100 percent cosmetic surgery.

Q. Why?

A. Doing so would allow us to avoid the increasing hassles with insurance companies and Medicare/Medicaid over coverage and charges for reconstructive surgery. As a cosmetic-only practice, there's no insurance involved. We're paid directly by our patients—cash or credit cards—or by companies that specialize in financing cosmetic surgery.

Yes, we're paid 100 percent in advance. We have virtually no receivables.

Our vision for Regency has always been to enhance our patients' self-esteem and success by improving their appearance. We believe our patients lead more fulfilling lives, both personally and economically, as a result of our treatment. We base this on the fact that so many of our new patients are referrals from former patients.

One of the first things we did when we took over the old practice was to retain Urban Contacts, a boutique marketing and advertising agency in New York. They came up with the name Regency, which we liked because it symbolized the high quality we aimed for in our practice. Urban recommended we limit our marketing activities to print media, rather than online, which they thought could cheapen our services. They said we shouldn't compete for viewer attention with the hundreds of ads people just scroll past. In particular, Urban recommended we advertise in what they called "Gucci glossies"—those slick, upscale magazines aimed at people with significant disposable income who are concerned with their image, the kind of people who shop at Gucci.

Urban suggested a couple of marketing themes that we rejected as too "cutesy." No, I can't recall what they were. Then they hit on "The Look of Love," which we really liked. Initially, we were concerned it might be illegal to use a song title for our slogan, but Urban assured us that no one can own rights to a title. They focus-grouped the slogan in connection with cosmetic surgery, and it got a good response, especially from upper-income people. So, they built our marketing campaign around the slogan. At first, it was limited to the Gucci glossies, but later, like everyone, we had to put up a website and that's searchable. We don't buy any online advertising. When we expand into new markets, we look for the upscale local publications in the area and that's where we advertise. We also expanded to theater and concert programs.

Urban took care of registering "The Look of Love" with the U.S. Patent and Trademark Office as our slogan.

Q. Please look at Exhibit 6. Is that a letter you received from Urban relating to registration?

A. Yes.

Q. And it specifically refers to Dr. Love?

A. Yes, but I don't think I remembered it when we moved into the Central City area. Our marketing goal was to establish Regency as a provider of first-class cosmetic surgery procedures. All our ads reference the kinds of procedures we perform and the fact that all our physicians are board-certified plastic surgeons, who are also members of the American College of Plastic Surgeons. Yes, our ads contain pictures of attractive people. No, of course the pictures in our ads are not pictures of our former patients—that would be unethical. The people in the pictures are models that Urban hires for photo shoots. I don't think they've ever used stock photos, but I'm not 100 percent certain.

The campaign has been very effective. Our New York City practice expanded to four surgeons within a couple of years, and, in YR-10, we purchased practices in Stamford, CT, and Saddle River, NJ. We paid for those practices with cash over time and Regency stock. In YR-8, we purchased practices in Buckhead, GA, and Naples, FL. In each case, the surgeons whose practices we purchased joined Regency, and, in each case, the gross and net incomes of the offices increased substantially. During the first year in each location, we achieved about a 10 percent revenue increase. After the first year, the practices showed annual revenue increases of 3 to 5 percent. We attribute the increases to higher patient loads per surgeon, better efficiency in medical and business practices, our ability to negotiate more favorable financial arrangements with the facilities at which we operate, and greater selectivity in the procedures we perform. Yes, we believe "The Look of Love" campaign is responsible, at least in part, for the increased patient loads, but how big a part I can't say.

Yes, the numbers were even better in Oakdale than in our other satellite offices. We increased revenues in Oakdale by 20 percent the first year, YR-6, and averaged about 8.5 percent in later years. We believe Oakdale did better than our other offices because, until recently, no other plastic surgery practice in the area engaged in any significant marketing campaign.

Yes, we still use Urban Contacts for our advertising. They do the artwork, find the appropriate media, and help us with online search utilization. For some years now, we've paid for a sponsor link on Google for searches that originate in the areas where we have offices and that use the terms "cosmetic" or "plastic" with the terms "surgery," "love," or "look."

The most frequent procedures Regency surgeons perform are facelifts; eyelid surgery; breast surgery, including lifts, augmentation, and reduction; body contouring; liposuction; tummy tucks; rhinoplasty; and injectables, such as Botox and collagen. No, not every Regency surgeon does each procedure, but every procedure is available at each of our offices. Our surgeons do not do laser skin procedures, dermabrasion, spider or varicose vein procedures, or small procedures like mole removals. We leave those to our physician assistants or we refer patients to outside specialties, most often dermatology, because those procedures don't require the training and experience of board-certified plastic surgeons.

In YR-6, we purchased Drs. Waters and Connelly's practice in Oakdale, a well-to-do suburb outside of Central City. Drs. Waters and Connelly wanted to slow down—they were both in their fifties—and they approached us about a possible deal. I negotiated the deal with them myself. I reviewed their books and their patient charts, inspected their office and the hospital where they operated, and talked to surgeons who were familiar with their work. Our businesspeople talked to their businesspeople. The whole due diligence process took about 120 days. We agreed to pay Drs. Waters and Connelly $500,000 each over a five-year period.

Yes, the issue of Dr. Love's slogan was discussed during that time. They told me Dr. Love was a local dermatologist who had used a similar slogan in cheesy online ads for some years. They didn't know much about Dr. Love's practice, but they were under the impression that cosmetic procedures were a small part of it and were limited to minor procedures like dermabrasion and mole removals. Dr. Connelly said Dr. Love and Regency couldn't be more different. "Like the Dress Barn and Saks Fifth Avenue" is how I think he put it. Dr. Connelly showed me one of the ads, and I agreed with that analysis. We briefly discussed asking Dr. Love to stop using his nonregistered slogan but decided it would be unwise for the new kid on the block to make waves. No, it never crossed our minds that using our registered slogan might violate Dr. Love's rights. No, our discussion about Dr. Love did not refresh my recollection of having received Exhibit 4.

Yes, Exhibit 10 appears to be an email exchange between Robert Connelly and me, but I don't specifically remember it. Yes, I understand you obtained it when you subpoenaed Dr. Connelly's records. No, we don't have a copy of it in Regency's records. We regularly purge all nonpatient-related emails that are more than three years old. Yes, I visited Drs. Connelly and Waters in Oakdale in November YR-5 as part of our due diligence. I have no reason to believe I didn't engage in that email exchange, but I just don't remember it.

Exhibit 11 is the website home page that we used for a couple of years. Urban designed it for us, and I approved it. No, the endorsements don't come from actual patients nor do the before and after pictures. We would never ask our patients to display themselves or to make public statements about their surgery. I think the copywriters at Urban wrote the endorsements and found the pictures somewhere. We reviewed them to make sure they accurately reflected our patients' feelings and results. No, I never intended to capitalize on Dr. Love's slogan in any way. I'm sure I never even thought about Dr. Love or his slogan when I approved the homepage. We stopped using the endorsement about "I love the look" after Dr. Love filed suit. Yes, that was after our lawyers in this case looked at the website.

When I got Dr. Love's email of September 13, YR-6, I was very surprised because we had registered our slogan and had been using it for six years without any problem. My first instinct was to ignore the email, but I sent it to Kal Foster at Urban. Kal discussed it with their trademark lawyer and gave me most of the language I used in my response to Dr. Love. Yes, Exhibit 7 is a copy of the email I sent. No, I did not intend that email to imply that we were competing with him for cosmetic surgery patients, but not dermatology patients. Based on what Dr. Waters had told me, I didn't think we were competing with Dr. Love at all. I intended simply to reassure Dr. Love we weren't trying to take his patients away from him.

I didn't hear from Dr. Love after my response, and I figured he was comfortable that Regency didn't pose any threat to his practice. So, I was shocked when, out of the blue, he sued us. Between the time I received his email and the time he filed suit, we probably spent about $120,000 in marketing our "The Look of Love" campaign in the Central City area.

I believe Dr. Love's claims are frivolous. We do different procedures, we're engaged in different specialties, and we advertise in different media. Yes, after Dr. Love filed suit, I did ask Dr. Waters if he knew of any confusion between Regency and Dr. Love. He told me that, on maybe three or four occasions, the Oakdale office received phone calls asking for an appointment with Dr. Love. Of course, that is second- or third-hand information. Dr. Waters told me that, on those occasions, the callers were given Dr. Love's phone number, which our receptionist knew from his ads: 1-800-LOVLOOK.

Yes, Regency's Oakdale office has been quite successful. Drs. Connelly and Waters are still practicing full time, and, as of the first of this year, we added a third plastic surgeon. Exhibit 8 is a summary of the Oakdale office financials since we opened it.

I know we have a Flashgram account, but I've never used it. Exhibit 12 appears to be that account, but I am not on social media. Kal Foster at Urban takes care of social media for us.

I have read the foregoing and certify it is an accurate transcription of my deposition testimony given on January 12, YR-0.

Drew Segan, MD
Dr. Drew Segan

Deposition of Jamie Anderson
January 15, YR-0

I'm Jamie Anderson. I live at 4285 Forest Street in Central City. I'm forty-nine years old. I'm a computer programmer with Atlas Engineering in Central City. I'm divorced and have three kids, two girls and a boy.

Yes, I've been a patient of Regency Plastic Surgery's Oakdale office. I had three liposuction procedures there in YR-3. I'd been divorced for three years and wasn't having much luck with the dating process. I'd gained some weight in my forties and thought my weight might be part of the problem. It seemed like liposuction would be the quickest way to improve my appearance, so I consulted with Regency and then I had the procedures. I also started a diet and exercise program at a gym.

I decided on Regency because I'd seen their ads in *Central City Monthly*. I called to see if they did liposuction. I made an appointment with Dr. Waters, who I really liked. I agreed to Dr. Waters's plan for three procedures. I've been extremely satisfied with the results.

Q. What was it about Regency's ads that persuaded you to call them?

A. They were professional and discreet.

Q. Is Exhibit 9 one of the ads you saw?

A. I can't say for sure, but that's the tone of the ads I saw.

Q. Was the slogan "The Look of Love" a factor in your decision to call Regency?

A. Not in and of itself. It was the ads in total.

Yes, before I called Regency, I had seen Dr. Stanley Love's online ads many times. I thought his ads were pretty cheesy. I had no interest in seeing a doctor who promotes himself online like a car dealer. I never considered calling him. No, I didn't know Dr. Love was a dermatologist. From his ads, I assumed he was a plastic surgeon because I thought that's who does cosmetic surgery.

I never thought the Regency ads in *Central City Monthly* might be ads for Dr. Love. The whole tone of Regency's ads was way above Dr. Love's ads. There's just no similarity at all. It never crossed my mind that "The Love Look" and "The Look of Love" were similar slogans.

I know that's true for other Regency patients as well. After I had my procedures, I joined a support group that Regency had formed, so we could help each other with our efforts to lose weight and keep it off. I went to meetings for about six months. More than once, we joked about Dr. Love and his cheesy ads. Everyone agreed they would never go to him for surgery. No one ever said they'd been confused between Dr. Love and Regency. There were about twenty people in the group.

I know two people who have been treated by Dr. Love. My daughter, Amanda, went to him for her acne about five years ago when she was thirteen. That was at the suggestion of her aunt, my former sister-in-law. I drove Amanda to her appointment and waited for her in Dr. Love's waiting room. After about twenty minutes, she came back to the waiting room in tears, all upset. All she could say was, "Let's get out of here." When we got outside, she told me Dr. Love was horrible to her—he called her a spoiled brat. She calmed down only after I promised she'd never have to see Dr. Love again.

My former sister-in-law is the other person I know who went to Dr. Love. She had him remove the wrinkles around her eyes and mouth. She thought she looked wonderful. I couldn't see any difference. I admit I was never particularly fond of my sister-in-law. She had her surgery done a couple of years before my marriage split up. She's a clinical psychologist, just like my ex.

Yes, my ex has remarried. No, I haven't.

Yes, I've been convicted of a felony. I was convicted of embezzling over $1,000 about seven years ago. I was initially charged with embezzlement over $10,000 from the computer consulting firm I worked for. I didn't embezzle any money; I just made a stupid mistake in a $15,000 overpayment to a hardware contractor. The problem was that the contractor was my old college roommate, and I made the overpayment about three weeks before he loaned me $12,000 to pay off a gambling debt.

I pled guilty because my lawyer told me that my story, even though it was true, sounded fishy, and I was facing a ten-year maximum sentence on the original charge. So, she plea-bargained a deal for me to plead to the lesser charge, which had an eighteen-month max. I told the judge I was guilty because my lawyer said it was the only way to get the plea deal. I was sentenced to six months in the county jail, plus restitution. I was released after four months because the jail was overcrowded. I made full restitution, even though it took a while. I've not had any trouble with the law since then. I had trouble finding work after that; it was hard because I had a felony conviction on my record, but I've had my present job for about five years and it's going well.

I have read the foregoing and certify it is an accurate transcription of my deposition testimony given on January 15, YR-0.

Jamie Anderson

Jamie Anderson

Expert Materials

Plaintiffs' Liability Expert Materials

Medical Dynamics

The Marketing of Medicine

Pat Brantly, MD, MBA
President

Mickie Quan
Quan, Warren & Rothschild
400 S. Ashley St.
Central City, Nita 80144

Greetings,

Thank you for sending this matter to me for evaluation.

You asked me to determine, from a medical marketing standpoint, whether potential cosmetic surgery patients are likely to be confused between Dr. Stanley Love's and Regency Plastic Surgery's marketing campaigns in the Central City, Nita, area.

To make that determination, I reviewed the depositions of Dr. Love, Dr. Segan, Casey Delp, and Jamie Anderson; the financial records of Dr. Love's and Regency's Central City–area offices; representative samples of Dr. Love's online ads and Regency's magazine advertisements; the parties' websites; and the survey that Survey Research Associates (SRA) designed and performed at my request. I base my opinion on those materials and on my medical and marketing training. I have seventeen years of medical experience in private practice, as well as eight years of experience in consulting with other physicians and medical practices about marketing issues.

2700 First Bank Tower
Chicago, Illinois 60611
312.555.5304

In my opinion, there is more than just a high likelihood that Regency's "The Look of Love" campaign might confuse patients; documented confusion has, in fact, occurred. Potential patients of Dr. Love have mistakenly called Regency's Central City–area office on many occasions. The only practical reason a patient seeking an appointment with Dr. Love would call Regency is that "The Look of Love" campaign led the patient to conclude that a call to the phone number in "The Look of Love" ad would reach Dr. Stanley Love's office. This explanation is confirmed by Casey Delp's testimony and by Dr. Love's testimony about the person he met at a charity function, who reported mistakenly going to Regency instead of to Dr. Love. This patient's experience demonstrates the damage done to Dr. Love: despite intending to use his services, the misunderstanding resulted in a patient having surgery done at Regency.

We know about this one case only because the patient happened to run into Dr. Love and tell him about this experience. We cannot know how many other patients who intended to see Dr. Love mistakenly made appointments at Regency. In my estimation, there have probably been a substantial number because these patients asked for an appointment for a specific concern, not a specific doctor. In my lengthy experience of internal medicine practicing in a seven-physician office, many patients asked to be seen for a specific concern, not to be seen by a specific physician. Thus, if a patient intending to call Dr. Love's office mistakenly called Regency and asked for a facelift evaluation, the patient would wind up with an appointment at Regency. Indeed, Casey Delp continued to believe Regency was an office of Dr. Love's, even during the first part of their appointment, and the caller who first alerted Dr. Love to Regency's campaign assumed the Oakdale office was associated with Dr. Love. Other patients seeking Dr. Love could easily have come into Regency's offices and then just decided to stick with Regency's doctors.

My opinion is supported by the survey SRA performed. SRA designed the survey to test the likelihood of confusion between Dr. Love's "The Love Look" campaign and Regency's "The Look of Love" campaign. I instructed SRA to limit the survey to persons ages twenty-five to sixty-five because I found on the American Society of Cosmetic Surgeons' website that almost 90 percent of cosmetic surgery patients fall into that age range.

The survey shows there is a high likelihood of confusion, as question five makes abundantly clear. Moreover, question four reflects the actual confusion both Dr. Love and Dr. Segan discussed in their depositions. If 25 to 42 percent of potential patients assume "The Look of Love" advertisement is for Dr. Love and call the Regency office based on that misassumption, the loss of patients and revenue for Dr. Love is inevitable.

The question arises why Dr. Love is not able to identify more patients who made this error. But it is not surprising that we do not know the identity of any patients who mistakenly went to Regency and actually had surgery there. The identity of those patients is protected by law, including HIPAA, and by medical ethics.

Over the course of my years at Medical Dynamics, I have provided marketing consultation to more than 300 medical and dental providers in the Midwest, ranging from solo practitioners to groups as large as twenty. I have become all too familiar with the pernicious practices of multistate medical corporations such as Regency. Their principal goal is to grow themselves by taking patients away from long-serving, local providers, much the same way that "big box" stores have taken business from local merchants.

One of the most effective weapons in the multistate medical corporation's arsenal is the slick advertising campaign. That was certainly Regency's tactic in the Central City area. Even in the face of Dr. Love's early protest, Regency persisted in its infringing campaign. They even purchased a Google search monthly subscription that places their website at the top of any search for cosmetic or plastic surgery and the words "love" or "look." There is no question in my mind that Regency's infringement was willful, as you have explained the legal definition of that term.

I will be pleased to testify in this matter. My fee, as I believe you know, is $700 per hour for all activity devoted to this case.

Very truly yours,

Pat Brantly

Pat Brantly, MD, MBA

SURVEY RESEARCH ASSOCIATES

CHICAGO, IL

MAIL SURVEY CONDUCTED FOR MEDICAL DYNAMICS

345 Nita City-Area Residents (response rate: 64%)

Age Range: 25–65

1. Have you seen Dr. Stanley Love's online ad in which he talks about "The Love Look"?

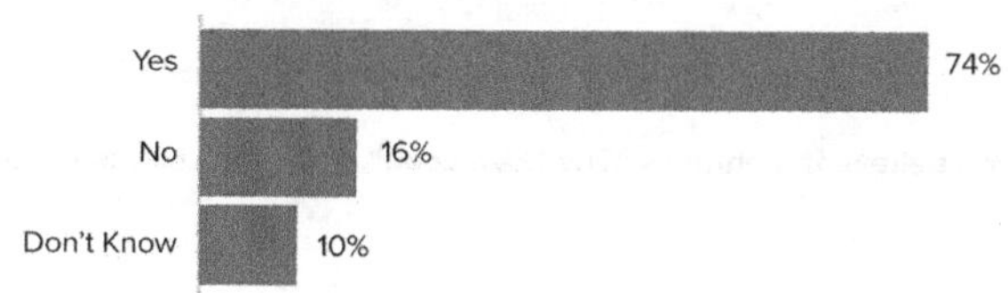

If your answer is "yes," answer Questions 2 and 3. If your answer is "no," go to Question 5.

---

2. Do you believe "The Love Look" refers to Dr. Love's cosmetic surgical results?

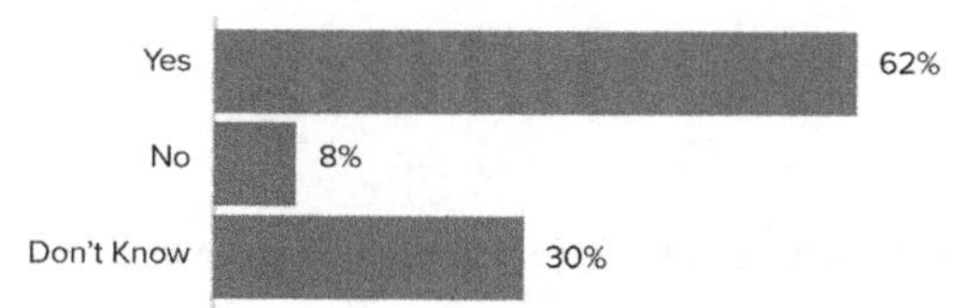

---

3. Have you also seen magazine ads for cosmetic surgery in which the phrase "The Look of Love" was featured?

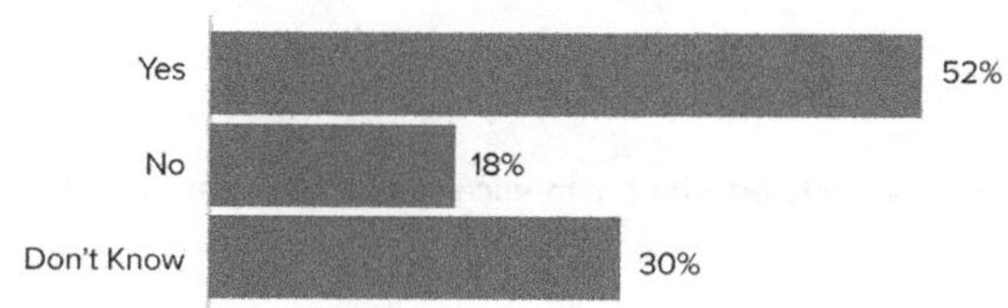

If your answer is "yes," answer Question 4. If your answer is "no," go to Question 5.

Mail Survey Conducted for Medical Dynamics

SURVEY RESEARCH ASSOCIATES
CHICAGO, IL

4. When you saw the magazine ads, did you believe "The Look of Love" referred to Dr. Stanley Love's cosmetic surgery?

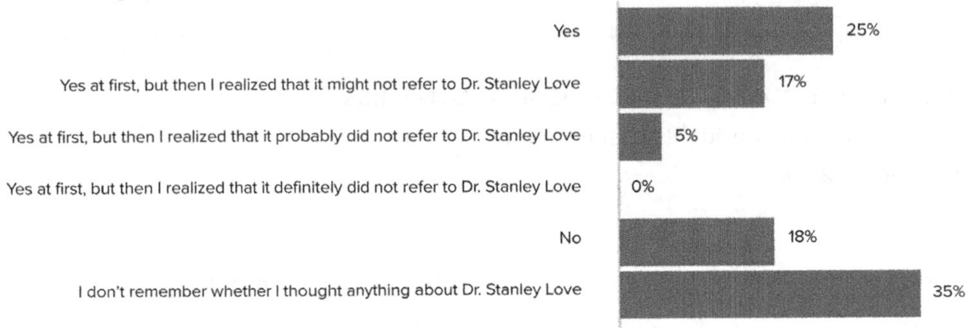

5. With reference to cosmetic surgery, do you believe the phrases "The Love Look" and "The Look of Love" are:

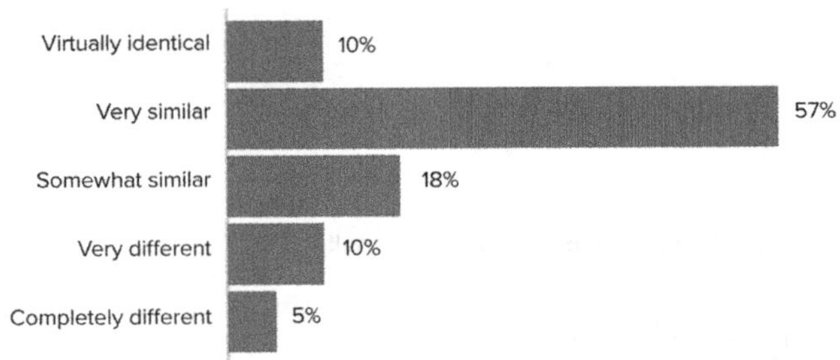

6. List the name(s) of any doctor(s) you assume are associated with the medical corporation entitled "Stanley Love, MD, PC":

7. List the name(s) of any doctor(s) you assume are associated with the medical corporation entitled "Regency Plastic Surgery, PC":

Pat Brantly, MD, MBA

Current Position

President, Medical Dynamics, Chicago, IL

Professional Employment

YR-17 to date	Practicing physician, Partners in Internal Medicine, Lake Forest, IL
YR-7 to date	Medical marketing consultant, Medical Dynamics

Education

YR-25	BA, Miami University of Ohio
YR-21	MD, Wight State University
YR-21–YR-18	Internal Medicine Residency, Detroit Medical Center (Wayne State University)
YR-8	MBA, University of Phoenix

Professional Organizations

Member, Illinois State Medical Society
Member, Lake County Medical Association
Member, American Medical Association
Member, American Association of Medical Executives
Founding Member, American Society of Medical Marketing Consultants

Publications

Eight articles on medical marketing (available upon request)

Expert Witness Retention

Retained in fourteen cases, all on behalf of plaintiff

Honors

Listed in *Chicagoland Magazine*'s "Compilation of Best Doctors," YR-17 through YR-1
Outstanding Resident Award, Detroit Medical Center, YR-17
Community Service Award, Chicagoland Chapter of ACLU, YR-4
Person of the Year, Chicagoland Toastmasters Club, YR-3

Certification

American Board of Internal Medicine

Defendant's Liability Expert Materials

Jean Woodward, PhD

4478 Silver Lake Rd.
Edina, MN

Ms. Alicia Robertson
Kilpatrick, Stone & Shah
1400 Vernor Ave.
Central City, Nita 80144

Dear Ms. Robertson,

You asked me to determine the likelihood of confusion between Dr. Stanley Love's "The Love Look" marketing campaign and Regency Plastic Surgery, PC's The Look of Love® marketing campaign. To that end, I have reviewed Dr. Love's and Dr. Segan's depositions and the Delp and Anderson depositions. I have also researched the field of cosmetic surgery, analyzed the two marketing campaigns, and conducted a survey and focus groups.

My survey was conducted by mail to Central City–area people, ages forty to seventy years. I chose that age range because my research revealed it is the most common one for cosmetic surgery. Potential participants were randomly selected using a professional survey platform. Participants were contacted by phone to determine if they were within the targeted age range and were willing to participate in a "consumer survey." We did not identify the nature of the survey. We assured each potential participant we were not attempting to sell anything, and their identities would not be revealed or provided to anyone. We sent the questionnaire to the 338 persons who agreed to participate, and received 264 completed questionnaires.

My analysis revealed that, although the campaigns' themes may seem similar at first glance, they are actually quite different. "The Love Look" is a phrase that is not in common parlance. Rather, it describes something that is unique to Dr. Love, either by identifying him as the doctor who performs certain surgeries or simply as an advertising slogan that makes clever use of his name.

The Look of Love®, on the other hand, is a phrase that is in common parlance; principally, because it is the title of a popular song that has been recorded by several well-known artists, including Dusty Springfield and Drew Krall. The phrase, largely as a result of the song's lyrics, denotes a look that conveys the emotion of love. It does not identify, directly or indirectly, a doctor who has performed surgery. The phrase, when applied to plastic surgery, is quite fanciful and quite different from "The Love Look."

The Look of Love® campaign makes it clear Regency's doctors are plastic surgeons. By contrast, as my survey demonstrates, fewer than half the people familiar with Dr. Love's ads believe he is a plastic surgeon. Thus, there is a greater likelihood of distinction, as opposed to confusion, relating to the sources of the parties' services.

Anecdotally, a small number of patients have mistakenly called Regency's Oakdale office in an attempt to reach Dr. Love. Because this insignificant number of mistaken potential patients had their temporary misunderstanding immediately resolved when they were given Dr. Love's phone number, there was no resultant loss of business to Dr. Love. My survey reveals there is virtually no chance that such a mistake would result in someone making an appointment with a Regency plastic surgeon rather than Dr. Love, let alone having surgery performed by a Regency surgeon rather than Dr. Love.

The parties, in the main, use different marketing channels. Regency uses print media aimed at a specific demographic (well-to-do adults), while Dr. Love uses online ads, which reach a much wider demographic. Although there may be some overlap, I believe it is not significant.

Finally, and importantly, I presented 2 fifty-person focus groups (with the same demographics as the survey group) with side-by-side comparisons of one of Dr. Love's online ads and one of Regency's magazine ads. Both were representative of their overall campaigns.

For one group, I presented Dr. Love's ad first, then presented an enlarged copy of a Regency ad. For the other, I reversed the order. I then provided the following questionnaire to the group members.

- I believe the online ad and the print ad are for the same doctors.
- I believe the online ad and the print ad are for different doctors.
- I can't tell if the online ad and the print ad are for the same or different doctors.

There was no statistically significant difference in the results between the two groups. In the first group, two people chose the first option, forty-four people chose the second, and four chose the third. In the second group, one person chose the first option, forty-eight people chose the second, and one chose the third. My conclusion is that this result demonstrates an extremely low (verging on nonexistent) likelihood of confusion.

Based on the above, I conclude there is an extremely low likelihood of confusion between Dr. Love's and Regency's campaigns. Therefore, I conclude Regency has not impinged on any common law trademark Dr. Love might hold.

I will be pleased to testify in accordance with my opinions. My fee schedule is as follows:

Review of materials: $400 per hour

Survey research: $500 per hour

Deposition testimony: $700 per hour (four-hour minimum)

Trial testimony: $7,000 per day (one-day minimum)

Travel: $350 per hour plus expenses (including business-class airfare)

Please call with any questions.

Yours truly,

Jean Woodward

Jean Woodward, PhD

Central City Cosmetic Advertisement Survey

Conducted by JeanWoodward, PhD

1. Have you seen Dr. Stanley Love's online ads in which he uses the phrase, "The Love Look"?

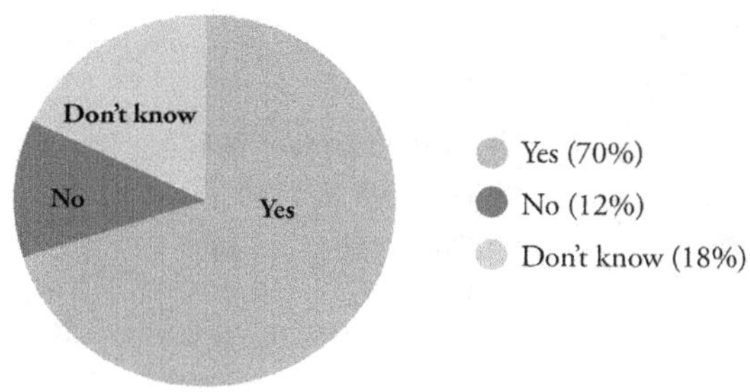

If your answer is "yes," answer Questions 2 and 3.
If your answer is "no" or "don't know," go to Question 4.

2. Do you believe "The Love Look" refers to:

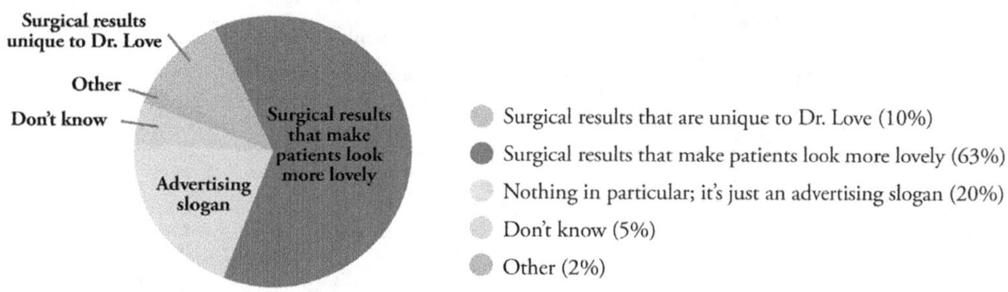

3. Do you believe that Dr. Stanley Love is a:

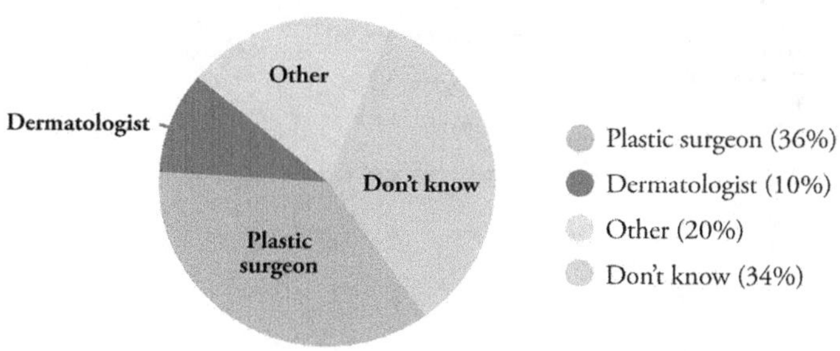

Central City Cosmetic Advertisement Survey

Conducted by Jean Woodward, PhD

4. Who do you think has more extensive training and experience in cosmetic surgery:

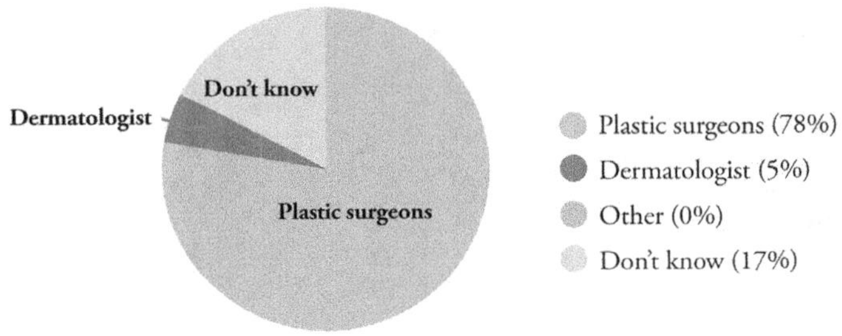

5. Have you seen Regency Plastic Surgery's magazine advertisements?

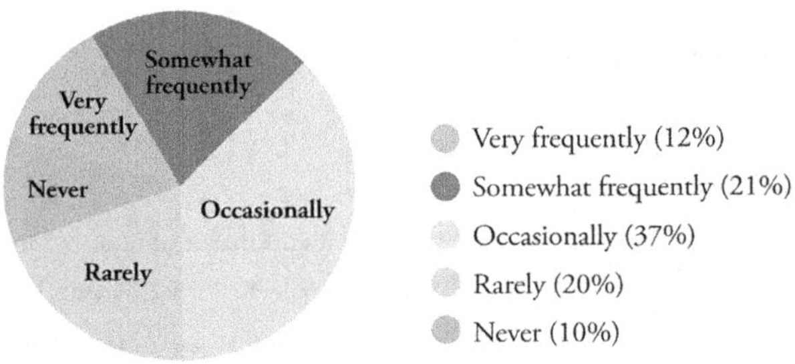

6. Do you believe that the doctors at Regency Plastic Surgery are most likely:

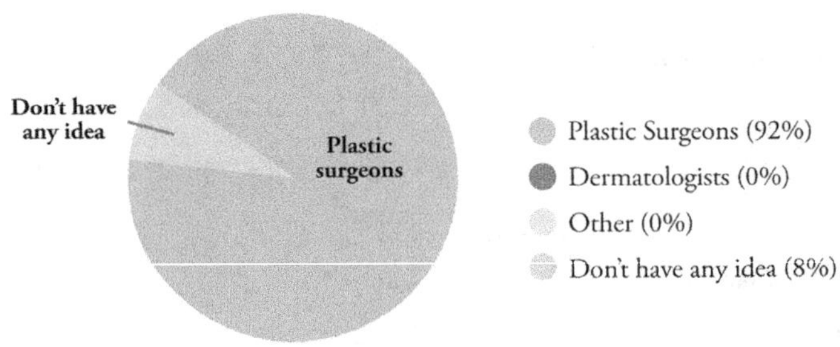

Central City Cosmetic Advertisement Survey

Conducted by Jean Woodward, PhD

7. If you intended to schedule an appointment with a specific doctor, but mistakenly called the wrong doctor's office, would you:

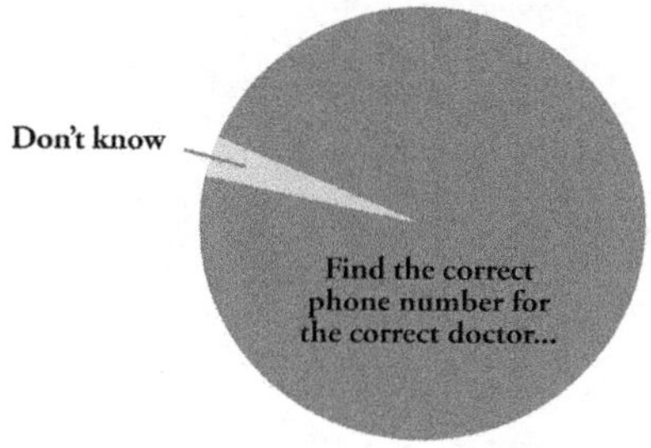

- Make an appointment with the wrong doctor (0%)
- Find the correct phone number for the correct doctor, and make an appointment with that doctor (97%)
- Other (0%)
- Don't know (3%)

8. Have you, or an immediate family member, ever had cosmetic surgery performed?

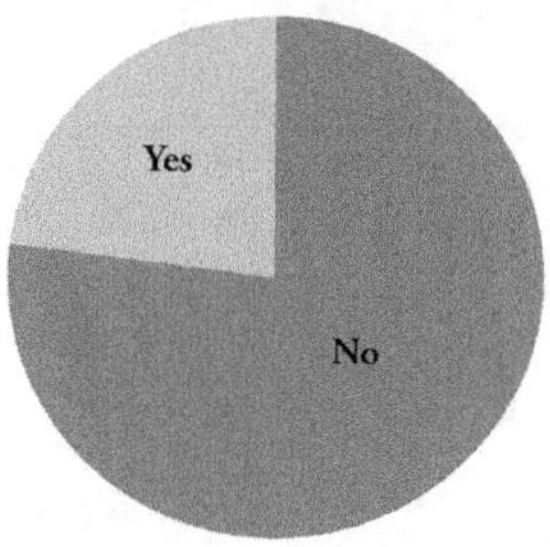

- Yes (23%)
- No (77%)

If your answer is "yes," answer Question 9. If your answer is "no," there are no further questions.

9. Who performed the surgery?

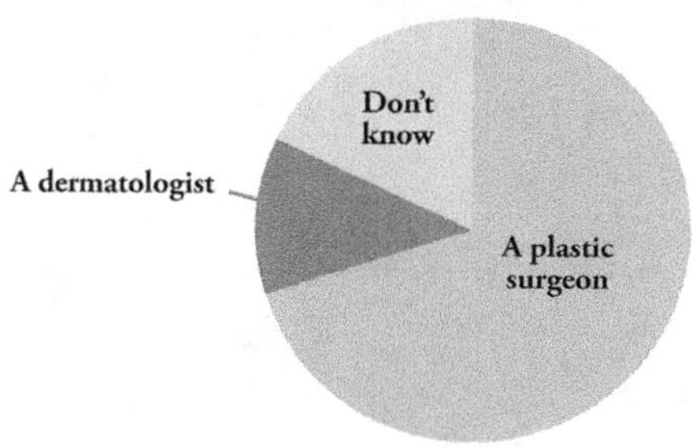

- A plastic surgeon (70%)
- A dermatologist (12%)
- Other (0%)
- Don't know (18%)

Jean Woodward, PhD
4478 Silver Lake Road
Edina, MN

Current Position	
YR-2–present	Rosenfire Professor of Marketing, Chair of Department of Marketing, University of Minnesota School of Management
Education	
YR-12 **YR-15** **YR-18**	PhD in Behavioral Psychology, University of Chicago MBA, University of Chicago BA in Psychology, Stanford University
Professional Employment	
YR-4–present **YR-6–YR-2** **YR-9–YR-6** **YR-12–YR-9**	Corporate consultation: Representative clients listed on Exhibit A Full Professor, University of Minnesota Associate Professor, University of Minnesota Assistant Professor, Northern Illinois University
Professional Organizations	
	Editorial Review Board, *American Journal of Marketing* Frequent Reviewer, *Journal of Consumer Research* Past President, *American Society of Consumer Marketing* Board of Directors, *International Marketing Society*
Publications	
	Thirty-nine articles on consumer marketing in peer-reviewed journals Two chapters in marketing textbooks Chief Editor, *Principles of Modern Marketing*
Expert Witness Retention	
	More than fifty cases, approximately 20 percent plaintiff, 80 percent defense
Honors	
	Lifetime Achievement Award, American Society of Consumer Marketing Outstanding Teacher Award, University of Minnesota School of Management Community Service Award, Minnesota Boys' and Girls' Clubs Voice of Reason Award, Minnesota Right to Life

Woodward CV Exhibit A

General Motors, Pontiac Division

CompUSA

Wendy's

Countrywide Mortgage

Minnesota Bar Association

American Academy of Plastic Surgeons

Circuit City

PepsiCo

NASCAR

Twin Cities Metro Transit Authority

Northwest Airlines

Allstate Insurance

America Online

Comcast

Altria

Borders Books

Plaintiffs' Damages Expert Materials

Forrester & Associates
Accounting and Bookkeeping Services
4220 Washington St.
Central City, Nita 80144

Mickie Quan
Quan, Warren & Rothschild
400 S. Ashley St.
Central City, Nita 80144

Greetings,

As you know, I have served as Dr. Love's accountant for more than fifteen years. I am quite familiar with his personal and professional financial records and have reviewed his and Dr. Segan's depositions, as well as Exhibits 4 and 7. I am familiar with Dr. Love's online ads. Additionally, as a subscriber to *Central City Monthly* and the Central City Playhouse Broadway Revisited Series, I am familiar with Regency's "The Look of Love" ads.

There is no question in my mind that Regency's ad campaign has adversely affected Dr. Love's cosmetic surgery revenues. This negative effect did not occur because Regency created new competition with Dr. Love. Regency merely replaced an existing competitor's corporate structure; the actual competitors (the doctors) remained the same. Thus, the only thing that can account for the dramatic increase in Regency's cosmetic surgery business is its advertising campaign.

I believe it took several years for Dr. Love to fully feel the effects of Regency's campaign. The small increase in his cosmetic surgery revenues in YR-6 is explained by the fact that many of his patients that year were completing a series of procedures they had agreed to before Regency started advertising in this area. Also, I know from conversations with Dr. Love that he frequently advises patients who have decided to have cosmetic surgery, but who do not have the money to pay for it, to contribute to a fund over time in order to accumulate the necessary sums. It's like a Holiday Club savings account. It often takes two or three years to accumulate the necessary sums. Thus, many of Dr. Love's YR-6 patients had decided to have Dr. Love perform their surgery before Regency started its campaign.

As a result of these financial factors, Regency's "The Look of Love" campaign did not directly impact Dr. Love's revenues until YR-5 when, for the first time, his cosmetic surgery revenues fell. The fact that his cosmetic surgery revenues have continued falling since YR-5, while his non-cosmetic revenues have increased, supports my conclusions.

From YR-8 to YR-6, Dr. Love's cosmetic surgery revenues increased at an average rate of 13 percent. If we conservatively assume that, absent Regency's "The Look of Love" campaign, Dr. Love's revenues would have continued at half that rate increase (6.5 percent) through YR-1, his yearly projected revenues, and the losses when compared to his actual revenues, are as follows:

Year	Projected	Actual	Loss
YR-5	347,297	313,700	33,597
YR-4	369,871	293,200	76,671
YR-3	393,912	279,700	114,212
YR-2	419,517	270,500	149,017
YR-1	446,785	250,400	196,385

Dr. Love's cumulative losses for these five years amount to $569,882. The average annual loss is $113,976. When that average loss is extended through the remaining eleven years of Dr. Love's work life to age sixty-five, the total future losses are $1,253,739 (11 x $113,976). I have not adjusted for inflation, nor have I reduced these losses to present value. My assumption is these adjustments would largely cancel each other out. Thus, the total past and future revenues lost because of Regency's "The Look of Love" campaign amount to $1,823,621. Historically, Dr. Love's salary has been approximately 28 percent of gross revenues. Applying that factor to Dr. Love's lost revenues, his total lost profits are $516,989.

Although I have never before testified as an expert witness, I will be pleased to support Dr. Love's case. My fees are my standard accounting fees, $300 per hour.

Yours truly,

Sammi Forrester

Sammi Forrester, CPA

Sammi Forrester, CPA

4220 Washington St., Central City, Nita ♦ (330) 555-3827 ♦ sforrester@forrester3827.nita

Education

Central City State College, BA in Accounting, YR-20

Employment

Forrester & Associates
- Director of Accounting, YR-5 to date
- Accounting Manager, YR-10–YR-5

Edwards & Greer
- Senior Accountant, YR-16–YR-10
- Staff Accountant, YR-20–YR-16

Civic Activity

Central City Rotary Club, YR-20 to date
Central City Lions Club, YR-20 to date
Central City Chamber of Commerce, YR-20 to date
Central City Choir, YR-12 to date
Central City Food Bank, Advisory Board, YR-3 to date
Boy Scouts' Brave Heart Trail Counsel
- Advisory Board, YR-10–YR-5
- Eagle Scout candidate mentor, YR-14 to date

Lawton School PTA
- Executive Board, YR-12–YR-8
- President, YR-10–YR-9

Central City State College Alumni Association, Trustee, YR-6–YR-2
American Muslim Society, Central City Branch
- Board Member, YR-7–YR-1
- President, YR-2

Central City Playhouse, Board of Trustees, YR-8–YR-4
Central City United Way, Executive Board, YR-7–YR-3

Educational Activity

Teacher, Basic Bookkeeping, Central City Community College, YR-5 to date
Saturday School Teacher, Central City Mosque, YR-18 to date

DEFENDANT'S DAMAGES EXPERT MATERIALS

Skyline Partners

Business Is Our Business

340 E. 63rd Street

New York, New York

Aaron Weinberg, CPA, JD

Alicia Robertson
Kilpatrick, Stone & Shah
1400 Vernor Ave.
Central City, Nita 80144

Dear Ms. Robertson,

I have reviewed the depositions of Drs. Love and Segan and the financial data contained in Exhibits 4 and 7. I have also researched the impact of new marketing campaigns on preexisting competitors and the impact over time of vanity online ads. Based upon my review and research, as well as my years as a CPA and business consultant, I have reached the conclusion that Regency's "The Look of Love" campaign in the Central City area did not adversely impact Dr. Love's cosmetic surgery revenues.

Regency began marketing in the Central City area when it opened its Oakdale office in January YR-6. The marketing campaign focused on Regency's "The Look of Love" slogan. It consists of ads in high-end magazines, such as *Central City Monthly* and *Hour Central City*, and in programs for the Central City Playhouse and Central City Symphony.

Over the first two years of the campaign, Regency experienced an increase in revenues compared to the predecessor medical office. Because the surgeons were the same, I attribute the increase, at least in part, to the campaign. Importantly, during the same period, Dr. Love's cosmetic surgery revenues were significantly larger than his cosmetic revenues prior to Regency's marketing campaign. Thus, there is nothing to suggest that Regency's campaign resulted in any damage to Dr. Love. To the contrary, my research has demonstrated that, when a new player enters a market, there is frequently an industry-wide increase in revenue. This is an example of a rising tide lifting all boats.

Here, the relevant industry is cosmetic surgery in the Central City area. It is my opinion that Regency's campaign increased public awareness of the benefits of cosmetic surgery and resulted in increased calls to all cosmetic surgery providers, including Dr. Love. Moreover, if there was any confusion in the public's mind between "The Look of Love" and "The Love Look," the confusion may just as well have resulted in people calling Dr. Love's office in response to Regency's campaign.

In YR-5, Dr. Love's cosmetic surgery revenues began to decline. The decline has continued to date. I believe the cause of the decline is that Dr. Love's ads became stale and far less effective. My research (printout from *Advertising Today Online* attached) shows that so-called vanity online ads (where a business owner or service provider is featured in the ads) are usually effective for three to five years, but much less effective afterward. In essence, the personality becomes stale. This is especially true where, as in Dr. Love's case, the character of the ads remains unchanged.

Based on my research and review of the available information, it is my opinion that Dr. Love has suffered no damage as the result of Regency's "The Look of Love" campaign. I will be happy to testify regarding my opinions. My fees are $750 per hour for research/analysis/preparation and $850 per hour for deposition and trial testimony.

Yours truly,

Aaron Weinberg

Aaron Weinberg, CPA, JD

Sign In Subscribe

Advertising Today Online

AGENCIES BRAND MARKETING COMMERCE MEDIA

Vanity Ads' Limited Lives

New Research Findings

by Olivia Lynch, staff writer
April 24, YR-3

For her MBA thesis at Emory University's Goizueta Business School, Courtney Levinson, 24, spent hour after hour watching so-called "vanity advertisements." These ads feature the very people whose products or services were being advertised. Ms. Levinson studied the ads of car dealers, injury lawyers, replacement-window manufacturers, dentists, tax preparers, furniture sellers, and for-profit college presidents in the Atlanta, Georgia area. She also interviewed twenty-two people who were in the ads or representatives of their companies. Promised anonymity, these people discussed, in general terms, their revenue histories.

Of the twenty-two campaigns, twenty resulted in significant (5 to 12 percent) revenue growth during the first three years of the campaign. The other two resulted in little or no growth and were discontinued within that three-year period.

ADVERTISEMENT

Looking at the twenty campaigns that showed significant growth, Ms. Levinson found that seven continued to show good growth (more than 3 percent) after the initial three-year period. The other thirteen showed less than 3 percent growth or no continued growth at all.

Without exception, the campaigns with good growth made changes in the character of their ads over the years (look, message, or both). The other thirteen campaigns remained largely unchanged for the period of Ms. Levinson's study.

Based on these results, Ms. Levinson concluded that vanity ads have a limited useful life, after which they provide no additional revenue. She found that, to remain effective beyond three years, the character of such ads must be changed.

I confirmed Ms. Levinson's findings by interviewing two prominent political consultants. They agreed that from one political campaign to the next—even if separated by only two years—a candidate's ad message must be changed.

Ms. Levinson will be submitting her thesis to marketing journals after she receives her degree. In the meantime, her advice to vanity advertisers is, "Keep it fresh."

Aaron Weinberg, CPA

EDUCATION

- BA in Accounting, University of Texas, YR-20
- MBA, Wharton School of Business, YR-18
- JD, New York Law School, YR-8

EMPLOYMENT

- Skyline Partners, New York City
  - Litigation Support Partner, YR-8 to date
    Testified in deposition or trial on damages issues in more than100 cases involving business disputes
  - Accounting Partner, YR-12–YR-8
  - Accounting Associate, YR-15–YR-12

Skyline Partners provides business and litigation support services through its eight domestic and three international offices. Skyline employs over 300 business, accounting, and legal professionals.

- Goldman, Sachs, New York City,
  - Financial Accounting, YR-18–YR-15

LICENSES

- CPA, YR-18 to date
- State Bar of New York, YR-7 to date

COMMUNITY SERVICE

- Member, New York City Firefighters Pension Board, YR-6 to date
- Congregation Beth Shalom, New York City
  - Board Member, YR-4 to date
  - President, YR-2 to date
- Advisory Board Member, New York City Marathon, YR-14–YR-8
- Board Member, New York City Chamber of Commerce, YR-12–YR-9
- Board Member, The Ronald Reagan Society, YR-10–YR-6

EDUCATIONAL ACTIVITIES

- Adjunct Professor of Accounting, City College of New York, YR-8 to date
- Frequent lecturer, School for Persuasive Expert Witnesses, YR-4 to date

EXHIBITS

Electronic copies of all exhibits can be found at the following website:

http://bit.ly/1P20Jea
Password: Love3

Exhibit 1

Dr. Stanley Love Online Ad

Commercial can be viewed at the following website:

http://bit.ly/1P20Jea
Password: Love3

Exhibit 2

"The Love Look" Brochure

Cosmetic Procedures Available in Our Office

- Eyelid surgery
- Lip augmentation
- Dermabrasion
- Collagen and other filler injections
- Botox
- Spider vein therapy
- Skin resurfacing
- Chemical peels
- Liposuction
- Laser treatments

Dr. Stanley Love is a board-certified dermatologist and a Fellow of the American Academy of Cosmetic Surgery.

What is the American Academy of Cosmetic Surgery?

The American Academy of Cosmetic Surgery is a professional medical society whose members are dedicated to patient safety and physician education in cosmetic surgery.

How to find us

"The Love Look"

Dr. Stanley Love, MD, PC
Dermatology and Cosmetic Surgery
"The Love Look"
3345 Richton
Central City, Nita

Hours by Appointment
1-800-LOVLOOK
(1-800-568-5665)

"Cosmetic Surgery – you owe it to yourself"

Exhibit 2 cont.

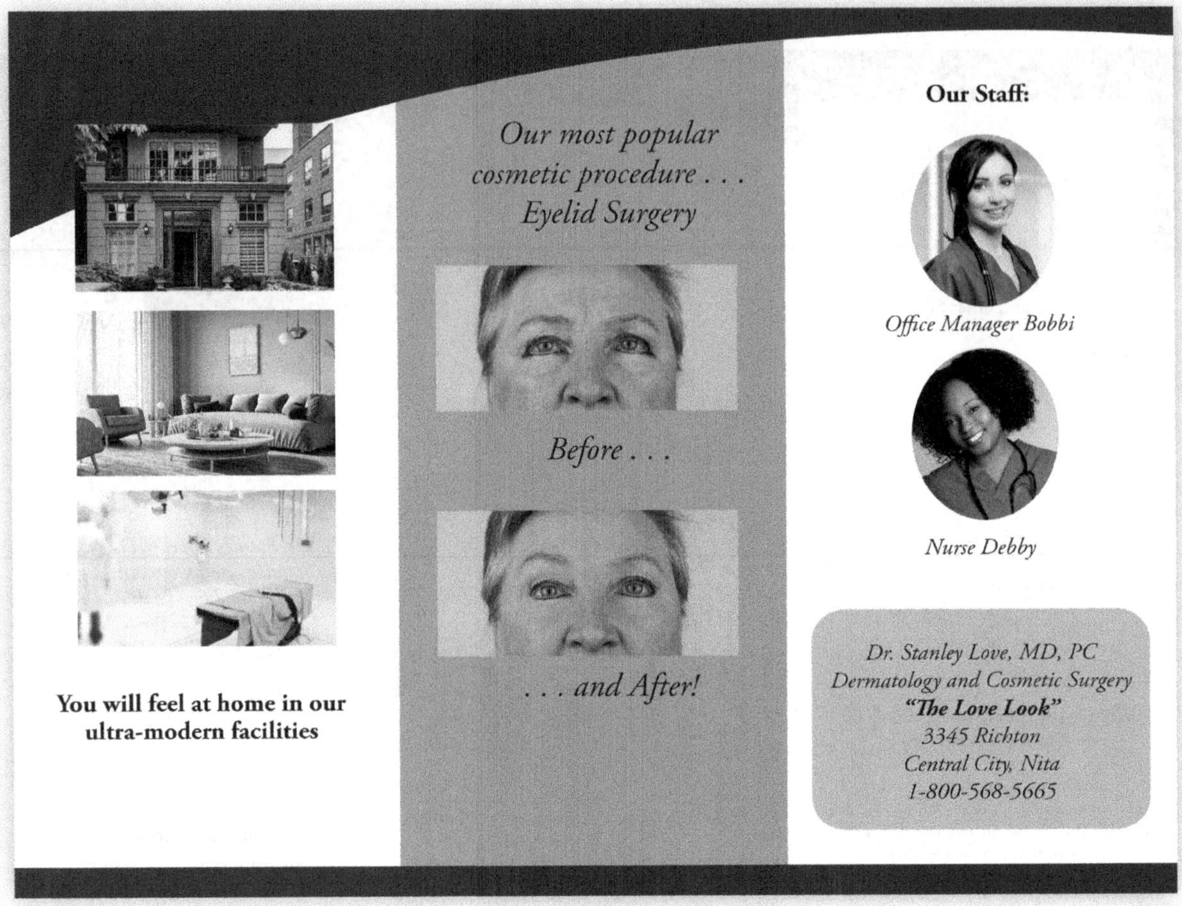

Exhibit 3

Dr. Love's Website

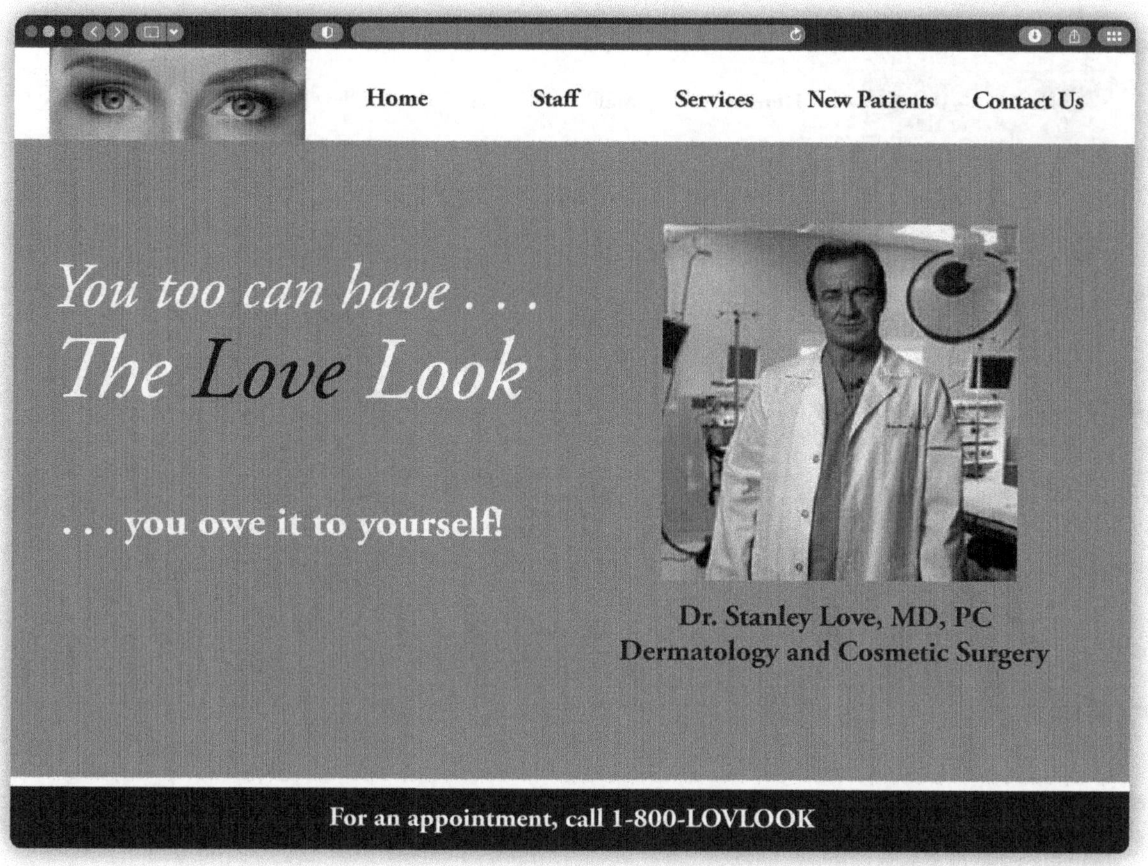

Exhibit 3 cont.

Dr. Love's Website

Exhibit 3 cont.

Dr. Love's Website

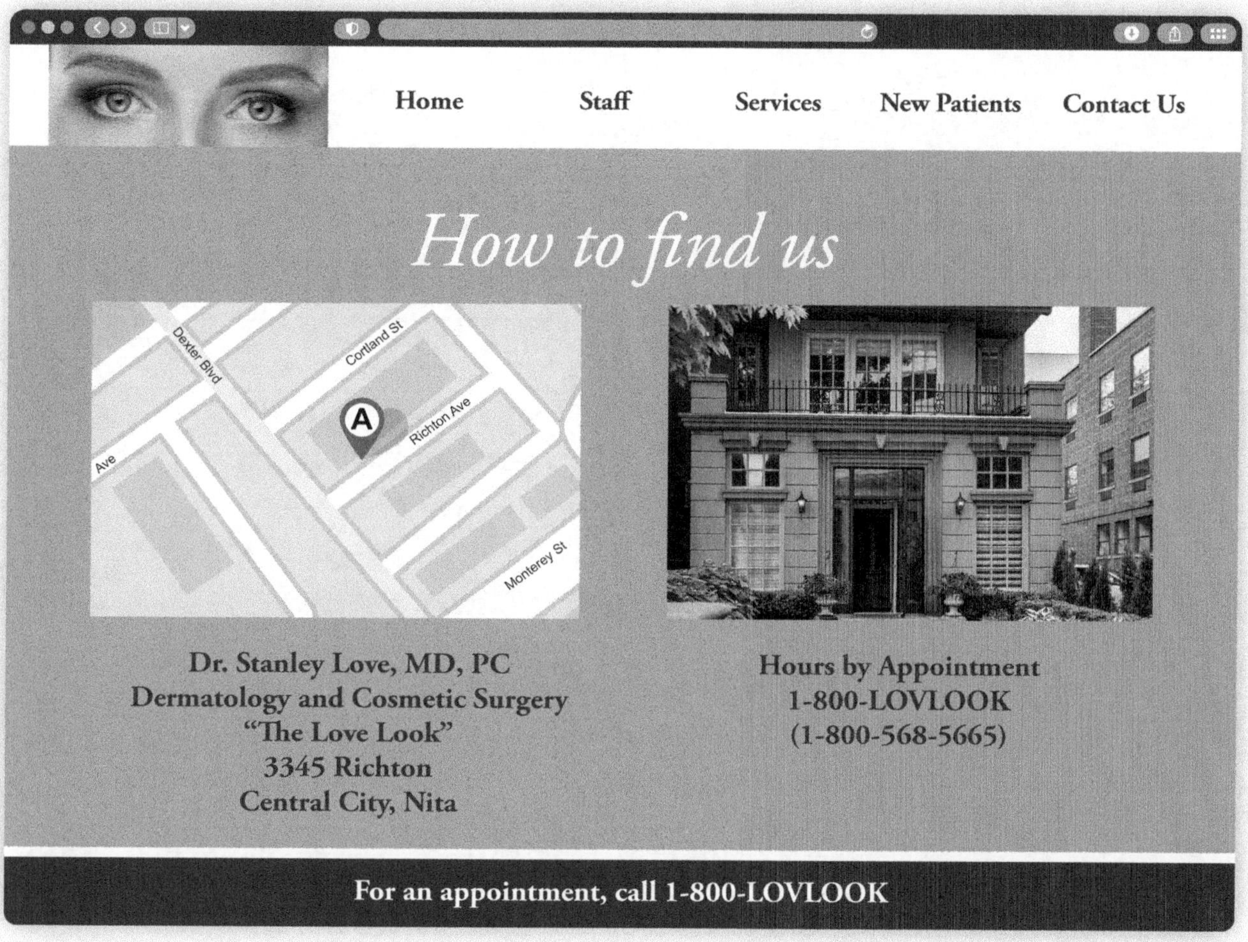

Exhibit 4

Email from Dr. Love to Dr. Segan

Stanley Love

From:	slove1@nitamail.nita
Sent:	September 13, YR-6 5:27 p.m.
To:	dsegan@regencyplastics.nita
Subject:	Your unethical slogan

Dear Dr. Segan,

For many years, I have successfully practiced dermatology and cosmetic surgery in Central City. Since YR-14, I have used "The Love Look" to promote the cosmetic surgery part of my practice. I am associated with the slogan and the slogan is associated with me.

I have invested many thousands of dollars in this promotion. I believe that Regency's use of my name and an almost identical slogan capitalizes on my investment and reputation and constitutes an unfair and unethical business practice. I respectfully insist that you cease and desist.

I am relying on you to do the right thing.

Yours truly,

Stanley Love, MD

Exhibit 5

Revenue Report for Dr. Stanley Love, MD, PC

Medisoft Report Generator • Stanley Love, MD PC

Cosmetic	YR-8	YR-7	YR-6	YR-5	YR-4	YR-3	YR-2	YR-1
Bleph Lower	26,600	28,200	30,700	28,400	26,000	24,000	23,200	24,000
Bleph Upper	36,100	42,400	40,200	38,000	33,000	29,900	26,700	25,500
Bleph Both	0	14,000	18,800	20,200	19,800	18,100	18,900	17,000
Botox	23,100	25,000	26,000	23,400	25,800	20,300	19,600	17,500
ChemPeel	17,600	10,800	13,800	18,400	15,400	16,800	22,000	20,800
Dermabras	18,000	21,500	20,500	21,600	23,100	23,400	21,500	22,200
Filler Inj	13,200	15,000	19,600	18,500	14,000	17,900	13,400	12,000
Laser Resrf Face	22,000	25,000	33,000	29,500	24,600	31,800	26,700	24,400
Lipo x1	60,800	63,200	65,100	63,500	61,500	50,400	49,900	44,100
Lipo x2	20,200	24,800	30,200	28,100	26,200	18,600	17,700	14,900
Lipo x3	0	2,800	6,200	6,500	5,200	6,200	6,500	6,400
Spider Vein Laser	17,600	15,200	22,000	17,600	18,600	22,300	24,400	21,600
Total Cosmetic	**255,200**	**287,900**	**326,100**	**313,700**	**293,200**	**279,700**	**270,500**	**250,400**
Total Non-cosmetic	**365,200**	**377,900**	**362,000**	**344,400**	**344,600**	**368,900**	**377,300**	**378,100**
Total Revenue	**620,400**	**665,800**	**688,100**	**658,100**	**637,800**	**648,600**	**647,800**	**628,500**
Expense Category								
Rent	88,000	88,000	92,000	92,000	100,000	100,000	108,000	108,000
Salaries & benefits	190,000	194,600	205,250	178,000	133,900	137,800	138,000	140,000
Advertising	54,000	55,000	57,500	54,600	52,700	55,200	48,600	53,500
Office admin	57,524	65,214	80,546	82,157	84,600	98,450	98,800	94,320
Dr. Love salary	175,000	225,000	205,000	190,000	170,000	170,000	175,000	165,000
Medical supplies	32,845	38,954	46,925	72,654	94,714	74,561	69,417	70,417
Total Expenses	**597,369**	**666,768**	**687,221**	**669,411**	**635,914**	**636,011**	**637,817**	**631,237**

Exhibit 6

Letter from Urban Contacts

Urban Contacts

430 Broadway
New York, NY 10012
212.555.4747

May 6, YR-13

<u>**BY MESSENGER**</u>

Drew Segan, MD
Regency Plastic Surgery, PC
341 E. 66th Street
New York, NY

Dear Drew:

Hope you are well. We've completed our research on "The Look of Love," and I'm pleased to report that there are no significant conflicts out there. Other than a couple of clothing and makeup lines, a wedding planner, and an online dating service, there are only two issues that could even remotely be deemed as significant:

First, a columnist in the San Francisco Bay area calls herself the "Love Doctor." Her column in the *East Bay Express* is called "The Look of Love" and offers relationship advice. The *East Bay Express* is a free newspaper with a limited local circulation. This has no bearing for us.

Second, a dermatologist, Dr. Stanley Love, in Central City, Nita, uses the term "The Love Look" to describe his practice in online ads. "The Love Look" is not registered with the state or the feds. Dr. Love has not trademarked his slogan. He is not a plastic surgeon, and his practice is geographically remote from Regency's. Our trademark counsel has therefore assured us that his use of a similar phrase will not prevent our registering "The Look of Love" with the U.S. Patent and Trademark Office.

Based on this research, we will move forward to register "The Look of Love" with the U.S. Patent and Trademark Office as Regency's service mark. This registration means that Regency will have the exclusive, nationwide right to this slogan for cosmetic plastic surgery services. Registration should be complete within sixty days. Once that occurs, please make sure that Regency always displays the ® symbol with its use of the slogan.

We feel confident we can now proceed with "The Look of Love" campaign. I've enclosed three ad mockups for you to consider. We'll need your go-ahead within the week if we are to adhere to the schedule.

By the way, I have a new restaurant for you to try: Rome Commune—it's in the West Village and quite good. Maybe I'll take you for lunch to celebrate the kickoff of "The Look of Love"!

Talk to you soon.

Sincerely,

Kal Foster

Kal Foster
Account Supervisor

Exhibit 7

Email from Dr. Segan to Dr. Love

Stanley Love

From:	Drew Segan, MD [dsegan@regencyplastics.nita]
Sent:	October 6, YR-6 10:14 a.m.
To:	slove1@nitamail.nita
Subject:	Re: Your inappropriate slogan

Dear Dr. Love,

Your email surprised me because we have never used "The Love Look" in our marketing. Rather, we have used The Look of Love®, which has been the registered service mark for Regency Plastic Surgery, PC, for more than six years. A simple check with the U.S. Patent and Trademark Office would have revealed that to you.

Regency has expended substantial resources in marketing The Look of Love® concept in the Central City area and elsewhere. We believe it is symbolic of the services we provide to our patients. We intend to continue our marketing campaign.

You may rest assured that we have no intention of using your slogan or extending our campaign to online ads, which, I am told, is your medium of choice. We will not compete with you for online presence or for your dermatology patients.

I wish you continued success in your dermatology practice.

Yours,

Drew Segan, M.D.

President
Regency Plastic Surgery, PC
341 E. 66th Street
New York, NY
regencyplastics.nita

> On September 13, YR-6 at 5:27 p.m., slove1@nitamail.nita wrote:
>
> Dear Dr. Segan,
>
> For many years, I have successfully practiced dermatology and cosmetic surgery in Central City. Since YR-14, I have used "The Love Look" to promote the cosmetic surgery part of my practice. I am associated with the slogan and the slogan is associated with me.

I have invested many thousands of dollars in this promotion. I believe that Regency's use of my name and an almost identical slogan capitalizes on my investment and reputation and constitutes an unfair and unethical business practice. I respectfully insist that you cease and desist.

I am relying on you to do the right thing.

Yours truly,
Stanley Love, MD

Exhibit 8

Revenue Report for Regency Plastic Surgery, PC

Regency Plastic Surgery
Yearly Procedure Productivity YR-6–YR-1
Office 6 (Oakdale)

Procedure Revenue	YR-6	YR-5	YR-4	YR-3	YR-2	YR-1
Abdominoplasty	81,200	92,000	102,400	110,800	124,400	129,700
Augmentation mammoplasty	140,300	145,900	182,700	196,700	220,100	228,200
Blepharoplasty	180,200	188,300	191,600	199,400	212,400	218,200
Botox	71,900	79,925	117,875	124,300	132,800	138,300
Breast implant removal	31,200	35,200	38,400	42,500	47,400	59, 200
Endobrow lift	0	32,800	38,800	41,000	48,100	52,300
Chemical peel	0	38,400	67,200	73,000	80,800	88,000
Dermabrasion	0	55,000	59,200	66,000	73,000	84,400
Facial implant	25,300	29,400	60,900	73,500	76,400	69,300
Inj–collagen	26,000	33,750	39,250	48,300	55,100	57,300
Inj–radiance	28,800	30,625	37,500	42,200	49,800	51,800
Inj–restylane	31,875	36,000	47,400	54,600	48,000	54,800
Laser hair removal	0	5,400	9,450	21,600	22,800	23,200
Laser resurface	0	48,600	66,800	77,000	82,500	84,000
Lip augmentation	0	17,600	42,800	51,400	59,000	72,400
Liposuction	304,700	322,000	325,900	322,900	324,000	328,400
Mastopexy	184,200	197,600	223,700	227,600	232,000	239,600
Reduction mammoplasty	92,400	72,600	88,800	91,300	103,300	99,000
Rhinoplasty	392,800	421,200	422,200	450,800	458,900	467,500
Rhytidectomy	688,200	702,200	765,000	770,300	781,200	784,300
Sclerotherapy	0	19,250	28,700	72,600	81,000	83,400
Totals	**2,279,075**	**2,603,750**	**2,956,575**	**3,157,800**	**3,313,000**	**3,354,100**
Revenue increase over previous year	20.00%	14.25%	13.55%	6.81%	4.91%	1.24%
Expense Category	**YR-6**	**YR-5**	**YR-4**	**YR-3**	**YR-2**	**YR-1**
Rent	215,728	210,600	210,600	210,600	221,700	221,700
Non-professional compensation	104,417	138,478	139,456	138,174	141,002	163,122

Office admin	54,123	41,879	43,458	42,745	48,415	51,471
Advertising	120,000	124,000	132,000	134,000	138,000	144,000
Professional compensation	1,000,000	1,200,000	1,300,000	1,400,000	1,500,000	1,700,000
Equipment and supplies	144,200	132,500	128,900	130,200	136,200	140,000
Totals	**1,638,468**	**1,847,457**	**1,954,414**	**2,055,719**	**2,185,317**	**2,420,293**
Gross Profit	640,607	756,293	1,002,161	1,102,081	1,127,683	933,807
Gross Profit Margin	28.11%	29.05%	33.90%	34.90%	34.04%	27.84%

Regency's "The Look of Love" Magazine Advertisement

Exhibit 10

Emails between Drs. Segan and Connelly

Robert Connelly

From:	Drew Segan, MD [dsegan@regencyplastics.nita]
Sent:	November 17, YR-7 9:40 p.m.
To:	Connelly, Robert [rconnelly@w&c.mds.nita]
Subject:	Re: Dr. Love

Thanks, Bob. I'm much relieved.

Drew

From:	Connelly, Robert [rconnelly@w&c.mds.nita]
Sent:	November 17, YR-7 9:05 p.m.
To:	Drew Segan, MD [dsegan@regencyplastics.nita]
Subject:	Re: Dr. Love

Drew:

Given our anticipated upscale, sophisticated patient population, I can't imagine that anyone will think that Stan Love is associated with Regency.

As to competition, although we and Stan offer many of the same services, I highly doubt his rather shoestring operation will take any prospective patients away from Regency. We'll have a much classier operation, in a much more desirable location (and you know what they say about location). If anything, we'll wind up with some of his prospective patients, not the reverse. But given the differences in the quality of our services, our higher fee structure, and the tone of our advertising, I doubt there will be any confusion.

I hope this allays your concerns.

Bob

Exhibit 10 (cont.)

Robert Connelly

From:	Drew Segan, MD [dsegan@regencyplastics.nita]
Sent:	November 16, YR-7 11:55 p.m.
To:	Connelly, Robert [rconnelly@w&c.mds.nita]
Subject:	Dr. Love

Bob:

I enjoyed meeting with you and Morgan, and I thank you for your hospitality. Please send my special thanks to Payton for the exceptional meal—particularly those amazing veal chops.

We should complete our due diligence very soon. I am quite optimistic that everything will be fine and that you'll be joining the Regency family in January. I have one niggling concern, however, and it has to do with Dr. Love in Central City and his low-rent ads.

We are very protective of "The Look of Love," and I want to make sure that, despite the similarity of our slogans, no one will think Dr. Love has anything to do with Regency. I'm happy to compete with him, but I don't want to be confused with him. Because you know the Central City area medical landscape, I need your reassurance.

Best,

Drew Segan, M.D.

President
Regency Plastic Surgery, PC
341 E. 66th Street
New York, NY
regencyplastics.nita

Exhibit 11

Regency Website

Exhibit 11 cont.

Regency's Website Page 2

Home | Our Doctors | Our Offices | Endorsements | Contacts

REGENCY PLASTIC SURGERY

The Look of Love

Our Doctors

BREAST | BODY | FACE | SKIN | GALLERY

OUR NEW YORK OFFICE

Drew Segan, MD
Board Certified: General Surgery
Plastic Surgery

Dale Tremble, MD
Board Certified: General Surgery
Plastic Surgery
Fellow: American Academy of Cosmetic Surgery

Amisha Kamar, MD
Board Certified: Plastic Surgery

Randall Jones, MD
Board Certified: Plastic Surgery

OUR STAMFORD OFFICE

Hal Woodward, MD
Board Certified: Plastic Surgery
Fellow: American Academy of Cosmetic Surgery

Rachel Levin, MD
Board Certified: General Surgery
Plastic Surgery

Rebecca Goldman, MD
Board Certified: Plastic Surgery

OUR SADDLE RIVER OFFICE

Joseph Rossi, MD
Board Certified: General Surgery
Plastic Surgery

Hanna Kowalczyk, MD
Board Certified: General Surgery
Plastic Surgery
Fellow: American Academy of Cosmetic Surgery

OUR BUCKHEAD OFFICE

Paula Grace, MD
Board Certified: Plastic Surgery
Fellow: American Academy of Cosmetic Surgery

Jeff Lanier, MD
Board Certified: Plastic Surgery

OUR NAPLES OFFICE

Ira Moss, MD
Board Certified: General Surgery
Plastic Surgery
Fellow: American Academy of Cosmetic Surgery

David Abelman, MD
Board Certified: General Surgery
Plastic Surgery
Fellow: American Academy of Cosmetic Surgery

Liya Almasi, MD
Board Certified: Plastic Surgery

OUR OAKDALE OFFICE

Carl Waters, MD
Board Certified: General Surgery
Plastic Surgery

Robert Connelly, MD
Board Certified: General Surgery
Plastic Surgery

Exhibit 11 cont.

Regency's Website Page 3

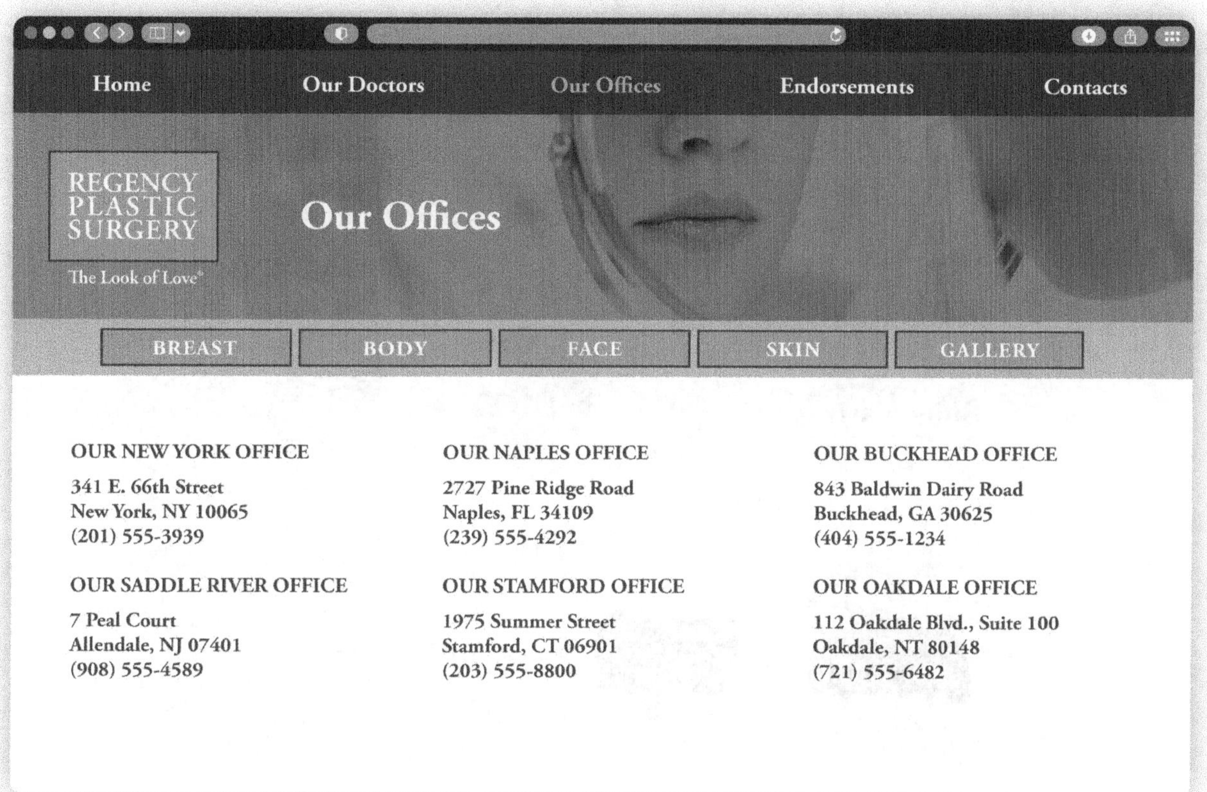

Home | Our Doctors | Our Offices | Endorsements | Contacts

REGENCY PLASTIC SURGERY

The Look of Love

Our Offices

BREAST | BODY | FACE | SKIN | GALLERY

OUR NEW YORK OFFICE
341 E. 66th Street
New York, NY 10065
(201) 555-3939

OUR NAPLES OFFICE
2727 Pine Ridge Road
Naples, FL 34109
(239) 555-4292

OUR BUCKHEAD OFFICE
843 Baldwin Dairy Road
Buckhead, GA 30625
(404) 555-1234

OUR SADDLE RIVER OFFICE
7 Peal Court
Allendale, NJ 07401
(908) 555-4589

OUR STAMFORD OFFICE
1975 Summer Street
Stamford, CT 06901
(203) 555-8800

OUR OAKDALE OFFICE
112 Oakdale Blvd., Suite 100
Oakdale, NT 80148
(721) 555-6482

Exhibit 11 cont.

Regency's Website Page 4

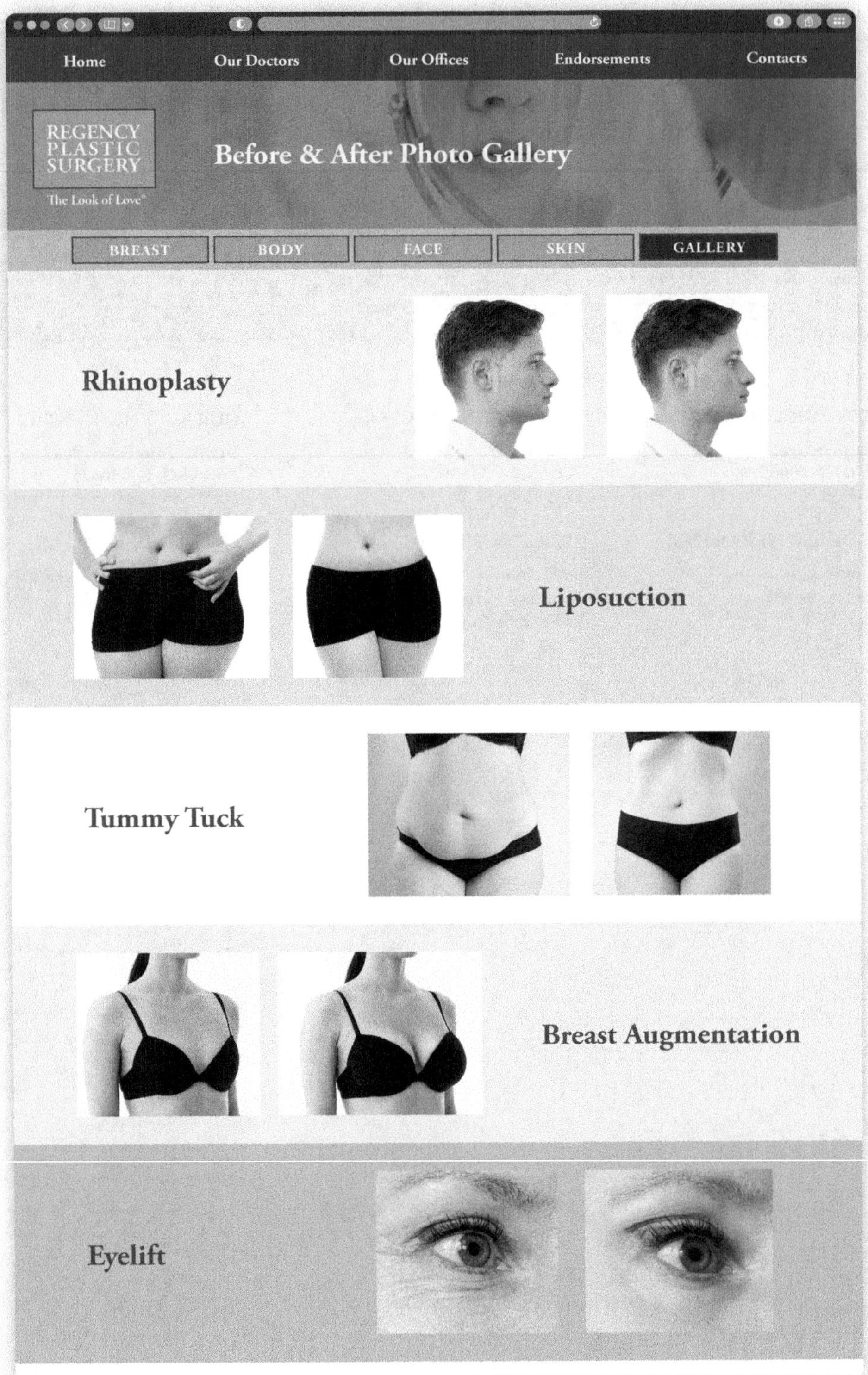

Exhibit 12

Regency Flashgram Account

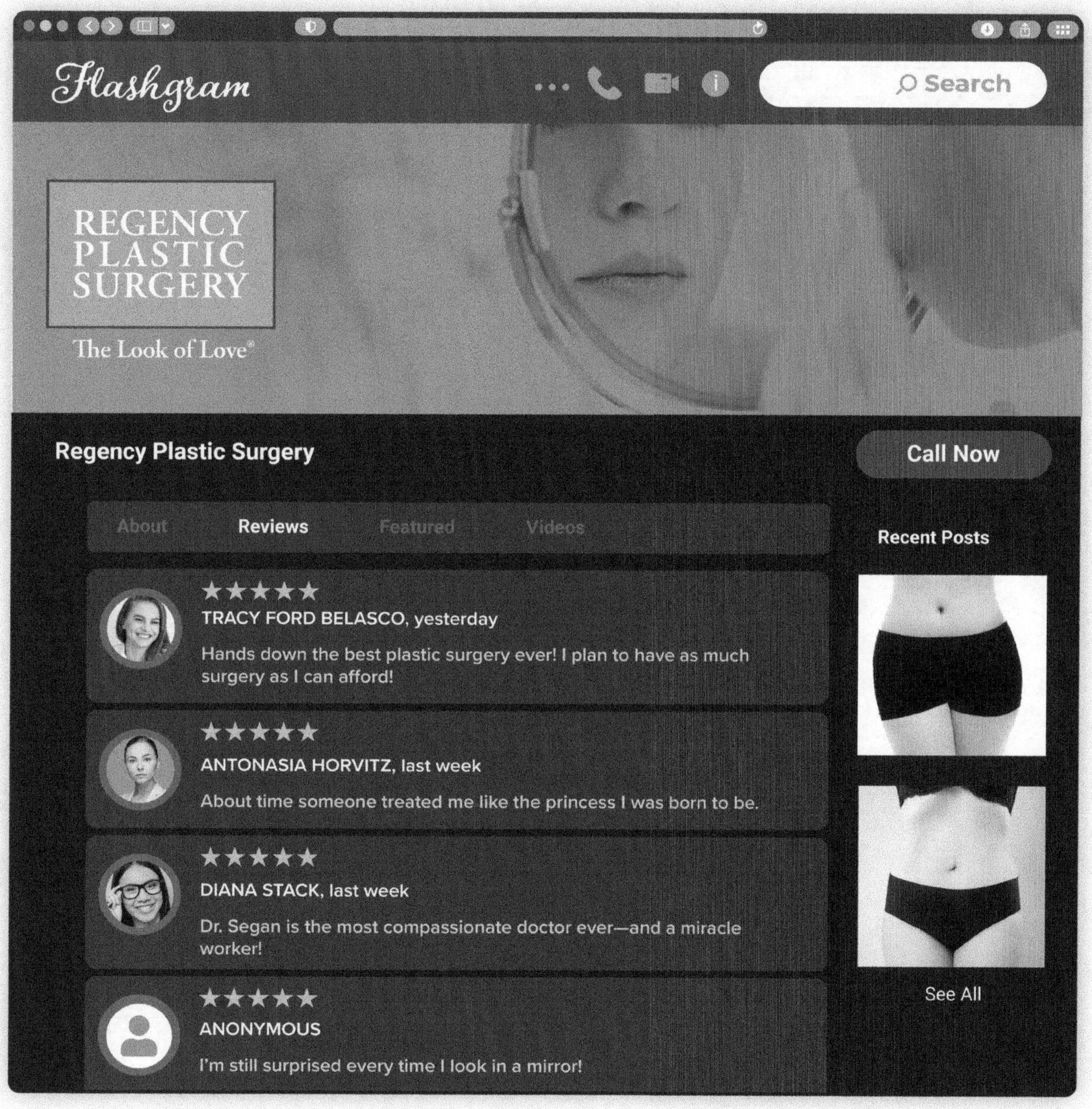

Appendices

SUMMARY OF APPLICABLE LAW

The Nita State Supreme Court has repeatedly held that usage in this state provides a common law trademark in an unregistered name or slogan, so long as the name or slogan is "fanciful," as opposed to merely descriptive. Thus, the Supreme Court has upheld "Purple Passion" as a common law trademarked name for grape soda pop but had denied common law trademark protection to "Good Old Grape Pop."

The Nita State Supreme Court has held that once a person acquires a common law trademark in a name or slogan in this state, that right cannot by defeated by another person's later registration of the name or slogan with the U.S. Patent and Trademark Office (USPTO). Such registration may provide the owner with rights in other states, but it does not affect a prior common law trademark in this state. On the other hand, once someone registers a name or slogan with the USPTO, no one else can thereafter acquire new common law trademark protection in any state.

State law provides that one whose common law trademark has been infringed can obtain an injunction against the infringer. The test for infringement is whether the defendant's use of a name or slogan is likely (probable) to cause confusion in the public's mind between the plaintiff's goods/services and the defendant's. The Nita State Supreme Court has held that the following factors should be considered in determining the likelihood of confusion:

1. Strength (distinctiveness) of the plaintiff's name or slogan;
2. Relatedness of the goods or services provided by the parties;
3. Similarity of the name or slogan;
4. Evidence of actual confusion;
5. Similarity of marketing channels used;
6. Likely degree of purchaser care in selecting the goods/services in question;
7. Defendant's intent in selecting the name or slogan (e.g., whether defendant intended to capitalize on the plaintiff's mark);
8. Likelihood of either party's expansion of product/service lines to more closely resemble the other party's.

The Nita State Supreme Court has held that in determining whether to grant a preliminary injunction, the trial court should consider the following factors:

1. Plaintiff's likelihood of success on the merits;
2. Irreparable injury to the plaintiff if the injunction is not granted (this is presumed on a preliminary finding of likely trademark infringement);

3. Substantial harm to others if the injunction is, or is not, granted; and

4. Whether the public interest is served by the grant of an injunction.

A plaintiff may also obtain past and future damages for infringement. The measure of damages is the loss to the plaintiff, or profit to the defendant, whichever is greater.

A plaintiff can obtain treble damages and attorneys' fees where the trier of fact finds willful infringement. "Willful" is defined as infringement by a defendant who has actual knowledge that their actions are infringing on the plaintiff's common law trademark.

The statute of limitations for a damage claim in this state is six years. The doctrine of laches applies to a claim for an injunction. The Nita State Supreme Court has held that a court of equity, in determining whether the plaintiff is barred by laches, should consider, but is not bound by, the statute of limitations that would be applicable to a damage claim. One is barred by laches if they delay an unreasonable time in filing suit to enforce their rights, and the defendant is damaged by the delay. Unreasonableness is decided on a case-specific basis.

Medical Terminology

Abdominoplasty—"tummy tuck" surgery

Augmentation Mammoplasty—breast enlargement

Blepharoplasty—eyelid surgery to remove excess sagging skin

Botox—injection of dilute botulinum neurotoxin that causes partial facial muscle paralysis with resultant decrease in wrinkles of skin overlying paralyzed muscles

Chemical Peel—chemically induced shedding of the outmost layer of the skin (this is the outermost layer of dead skin cells)

Dermabrasion—procedure to remove skin imperfections by abrasion or "sanding"

Endobrow Lift—facelift involving the forehead

Facial Implant—placement of artificial material to enhance "bone structure," usually placed in the nose or chin

Filler Injections—injections of biologic material to fill unsightly depressions in the skin. This includes collagen, *Radiance,* and *Restylane*

Laser Hair Removal—procedure using a laser to destroy unwanted hair follicles

Laser Resurfacing—similar to dermabrasion, except that a laser is used to remove skin imperfections instead of a "sanding" technique

Lip Augmentation—injection of fat or other biologic material into lips

Liposuction—vacuum procedure to remove subcutaneous fat

Mastopexy—breast surgery to correct sagging

Reduction Mammoplasty—surgery to reduce breast size

Rhinoplasty—surgery to reshape the nose

Rhytidectomy—facelift surgery

Sclerotherapy—injection of a chemical irritant into spider veins, causing the veins to close and disappear

Spider Vein Laser—laser beam used to destroy spider veins

Spider Veins—small dilated (varicose) veins, which have the appearance of spiders directly under the skin

Medical/Surgical Credentialing

Dermatologists are physicians who complete residencies in dermatology and specialize in the care of the skin. To become certified by the American Board of Dermatology, one must complete medical school, an internship, and an approved residency in dermatology that lasts for three years beyond the internship year. One must also pass the certification exam given by the American Board of Dermatology. Dermatology residency typically includes training in a limited number of surgical procedures, some of which may be described as cosmetic in nature. Some dermatologists elect to undergo a dermatologic surgery fellowship. This additional year of training provides experience in cosmetic and cancer-related skin surgery. Upon completion, they are qualified to practice dermatologic surgery.

The American Academy of Dermatology accredits training programs in dermatology. It also confers fellowship status based, in part, on certification by the American Board of Dermatology. The American Board of Dermatology certifies dermatologists by administering an oral and written examination. The American Board of Dermatology is recognized by the American Board of Medical Specialties.

Dermatology—Years of Internship/Residency: 4

Plastic surgeons are physicians who complete residencies in plastic surgery and specialize in surgery for body modification and reconstruction. To become certified by the American Board of Plastic Surgery, one must complete medical school, an internship, and an additional three years of general surgery residency. A minimum of two years of plastic surgical residency are also required prior to passing a certification examination given by the American Board of Plastic Surgery. Plastic surgeons typically perform a larger number of more complex cosmetic surgical procedures, in addition to restorative surgery. These restorative surgeries are performed, for example, on cancer or burn patients.

The American Board of Surgery certifies general surgeons, while the American Board of Plastic Surgery certifies plastic surgeons. Both administer oral and written exams for certification. Both are recognized by the American Board of Medical Specialties. The American Society of Plastic Surgeons affords membership only to fully qualified plastic surgeons.

Plastic Surgery—Years of Internship/Residency: 6 to 8

Cosmetic Surgeons are physicians who have a strong interest in cosmetic surgery. There are no formal requirements to use the term "cosmetic" surgeon. The American Board of Cosmetic Surgery offers credentialing to physicians who complete residencies in dermatology, ear, nose, and throat surgery, as well as other specialties. These physicians may choose to become board certified in cosmetic surgery by completing an approved additional fellowship year in cosmetic surgery and up to 300 hours of continuing medical education in topics of relevance to cosmetic surgery (depending on other certification). Until 2008, physicians could obtain board certification by performing at least 1,000 cosmetic surgical procedures without completing a fellowship year. This pathway was eliminated in August 2008 in favor of an accredited fellowship. After completing these educational requirements, board candidates must pass a certification exam given by the American Board of Cosmetic Surgery. The American Academy of Cosmetic Surgery awards fellowship status to physicians who have completed at least one hundred cosmetic surgical procedures. This "fellow" designation is independent of board certification in cosmetic surgery.

The American Board of Cosmetic Surgery certifies cosmetic surgeons following a one-year fellowship (or completion of 1,000 procedures before 2008). The American Board of Cosmetic Surgery is not recognized by the American Board of Medical Specialties. The American Academy of Cosmetic Surgery accredits training programs in cosmetic surgery and bestows the designation "Fellow of the American Academy of Cosmetic Surgery" after completion of one hundred cosmetic surgical procedures (board certification not required).

Cosmetic Surgery—Years of Internship/Residency: Variable Depending on Other Certification

Jury Instructions

1. The law you are to apply to this case is contained in these instructions, and it is your duty to follow the instructions. You must consider them as a whole, and not pick out one or some instructions and disregard others.

2. Sympathy or prejudice must not influence your decision.

3. I have not meant to indicate any opinion as to the facts by my rulings, conduct, or remarks during the trial. But if you think I have, you should disregard it because you are the sole judges of the facts.

4. You shall consider all of the evidence bearing on any fact without regard to which party produced the evidence.

5. A fact may be proven directly by a witness or indirectly by other facts or circumstances from which it reasonably follows according to the common experience of humankind. This indirect evidence is called circumstantial evidence, and it should be considered by you in the same manner as direct evidence.

6. In determining which witnesses you will believe and what weight you will give to their testimony, you may take into account each witness's ability and opportunity to observe, their memory, manner while testifying, and any interest, bias, or prejudice they may have.

7. Plaintiffs claim that, because they were using "The Love Look" as their slogan before Defendant registered "The Look of Love" as its slogan, the Plaintiffs acquired a common law trademark in "The Love Look," which is superior in this state to the Defendant's later, federally registered trademark of "The Look of Love." In connection with this claim, Plaintiffs have the burden of proving, by a preponderance of the evidence, that the slogan "The Love Look," as applied to Dr. Love's cosmetic surgery, is not merely descriptive of his surgery but is a fanciful slogan—that is, a slogan used in an imaginative way. If you find that Plaintiffs have met their burden of proof, then you must find that their trademark is superior to (takes precedence over) the Defendant's trademark in this state.

8. Plaintiffs also claim that Defendant infringed on their trademark rights to the slogan "The Love Look." In connection with this claim, Plaintiffs have the burden of proving, by a preponderance of the evidence, that Defendant's use of "The Look of Love" would probably cause confusion in the public's mind between Plaintiffs' and Defendant's cosmetic surgery practices. In your determination of this issue, you should consider the following, to the extent that you find they are supported by the evidence:

a. The distinctiveness of Plaintiffs' slogan, "The Love Look";

b. The similarity of the services provided by the parties;

c. Any similarity of the parties' slogans;

d. Any evidence of actual confusion;

e. Any similarity of marketing channels;

f. The likelihood of purchaser care in selecting a cosmetic surgery provider;

g. Whether Defendant intended to capitalize on Plaintiffs' slogan; and

h. Any evidence of Defendant's expansion of its cosmetic surgery services to more closely resemble Plaintiffs'.

9. Plaintiffs also claim, and have the burden of proving by a preponderance of the evidence, that they have been damaged by Defendant's infringement of Plaintiffs' "The Love Look" slogan.

10. Your verdict will be for the Plaintiffs if they prove that:

a. "The Love Look," as applied to Dr. Love's cosmetic surgery, is not merely descriptive of his surgery but is a fanciful slogan (used in an imaginative way);

b. Defendant infringed on Plaintiffs' trademark rights to the slogan "The Love Look"; and

c. Plaintiffs have been damaged by Defendant's infringement of Plaintiffs' "The Love Look" slogan.

Your verdict will be for the Defendant if Plaintiffs fail to prove any of these elements.

11. If you find that the Plaintiffs are entitled to damages, you should determine the amount of money that will fairly compensate them for the following elements of damage, as proved by the evidence:

a. Plaintiffs' past lost profits or Defendant's profits from its infringement (whichever is greater), and

b. Plaintiffs' future lost profits.

12. If your verdict is for the Plaintiffs, you must also determine whether Plaintiffs have proved, by a preponderance of the evidence, that Defendant's infringement was willful. The term "willful" means that Defendant had actual knowledge that it was infringing on the Plaintiffs' trademark rights to the slogan "The Love Look."

13. I will furnish you with a form for your verdict. Please fill in the appropriate blank(s) when ______ of you agree to the answer.

14. Answer "Yes" or "No" to all questions that require a "Yes" or "No" answer. A "Yes" answer must be based on a preponderance of the evidence. If you do not find that a preponderance of the evidence supports a "Yes" answer, then answer "No." The term "preponderance of the evidence" means the greater weight and degree of credible evidence admitted in this case. Whenever a question requires an answer other than "Yes" or "No," your answer must be based on a preponderance of the evidence unless you are otherwise instructed.

STATE COURT OF NITA
COUNTY OF NITA

STANLEY LOVE, MD and STANLEY LOVE, MD, PC, Plaintiffs, vs. REGENCY PLASTIC SURGERY, Defendant.	)))))))))))	CIVIL NO. YR-1–CV–96369

VERDICT FORM
[trial on liability and damages]

We find as follows:

QUESTION #1: Is the slogan "The Love Look," as applied to Dr. Love's cosmetic surgery, not merely descriptive of his surgery but a fanciful slogan?

ANSWER: _________ [Yes or No]

If your answer is "no," do not answer any further questions.

QUESTION #2: Did the Defendant infringe on the Plaintiffs' "The Love Look" slogan?

ANSWER: _________ [Yes or No]

If your answer is "no," do not answer any further questions.

QUESTION #3: Were the Plaintiffs damaged by the Defendant's infringement of the Plaintiffs' "The Love Look" slogan?

ANSWER: _________ [Yes or No]

If your answer is "no," do not answer any further questions.

QUESTION #4: What are the Plaintiffs' damages for:

Past lost profits or the Defendant's infringement profits $_________

Future lost profits $_________

QUESTION #5: Was the Defendant's infringement of "The Love Look" slogan willful?

ANSWER: ____________ [Yes or No]

Signed,

Jury Foreperson

STATE COURT OF NITA
COUNTY OF NITA

STANLEY LOVE, MD and STANLEY LOVE, MD, PC, Plaintiffs, vs. REGENCY PLASTIC SURGERY, Defendant.	)))))))))))	CIVIL NO. YR-1–CV–96369

VERDICT FORM
[trial on liability only]

We find as follows:

QUESTION #1: Is the slogan "The Love Look," as applied to Dr. Love's cosmetic surgery, not merely descriptive of his surgery but a fanciful slogan?

ANSWER: _________ [Yes or No]

If your answer is "no," do not answer any further questions.

QUESTION #2: Did Defendant infringe on the Plaintiffs' "The Love Look" slogan?

ANSWER: _________ [Yes or No]

If your answer is "no," do not answer any further questions.

QUESTION #3: Were Plaintiffs damaged by Defendant's infringement of Plaintiffs' "The Love Look" slogan?

ANSWER: _________ [Yes or No]

Signed,

Jury Foreperson

IMPEACHMENT EXERCISES

1. Assume Dr. Love testified on direct examination that the first time he considered suing Regency was last year [YR-1] when his cosmetic surgery revenues continued to decline. Impeach him from his deposition.

2. Assume Dr. Love testified on direct examination: "I left a detailed message on Dr. Waters's voicemail that Regency was unfairly trading on my slogan." Impeach him from his deposition.

3. Assume J. Anderson testified on direct examination that "The Look of Love" slogan played absolutely no part in their decision to have surgery at Regency. Impeach them from their deposition.

4. Assume C. Delp testified on direct examination that when they mistakenly called Regency's office, they specifically asked for an appointment with Dr. Love. Impeach them from their deposition.

5. Assume Dr. Segan testified on direct examination that they absolutely did not recall Exhibit 6 when they were planning the Oakdale office or when they gave the go ahead to use "The Look of Love" campaign in the Central City area. Impeach them from their deposition.

6. Assume Dr. Segan testified on direct examination: "The reason Dr. Fostyk and I limited our practice to cosmetic surgery was first and foremost because we were emotionally burnt out after treating badly deformed patients." Impeach them from their deposition.

